THE WAR ON ISLAM

ENVER MASUD

MADRASAH BOOKS

An Imprint of The Wisdom Fund

THE WAR ON ISLAM
Copyright © 2000 by Enver Masud
All rights reserved.

Published by:
The Wisdom Fund
Madrasah Books Division
P.O. Box 2723
Arlington, VA 22202
USA
E-mail—wisdom@twf.org
Web site—www.twf.org

Publisher's Cataloging-in-Publication
(Provided by Quality Books, Inc.)

Masud, Enver.
    The war on Islam / Enver Masud.—1st ed.
    p. cm.
    Includes bibliographical references
    LCCN: 00–101893
    ISBN: 0–9700011–0–X

    1. Islam in mass media. 2. Mass media—
Objectivity—United States. 3. Mass media
criticism. 4. Islam—Public opinion. 5. Mass
media and public opinion—United States.
I. Title

P96.I84M37 2000
302.23/088/2971   QBI00–353

Printed in the United States of America

To my mother and father
who by example taught me the
values for which I strive,
but often fail, to live by.

To the editor, Mowahid Shah, and
publisher, Muhammad Aslam,
who gave me the opportunity
to write for *Eastern Times*.

And to many others
from whom I have learned, or
by whom I have been inspired.

Preface

It started with the Gulf War.

As an immigrant whose first formal education was at an American school in India, an engineering graduate of the University of Oklahoma who had witnessed the Watergate hearings, and an engineering management consultant who then had little interest in history or politics, it had never occurred to me to question the credibility of major U.S. media.

But media coverage of the 1991 Gulf War left me with a host of unanswered questions. Were Iraq and "Islamic terrorism" the threat they were made out to be? Why were the "rogue states" so described? What was this New World Order?

The more I read the more questions I had, and over the next few years I began to realize that the media were presenting half truths, and perhaps outright lies, designed to support official U.S. positions. The media seemed to be acting as public relations firms for the U.S. Department of State, rather than as neutral reporters or analysts.

I felt an overwhelming urge to present an alternative view, and began contributing article to a Washington area newspaper—*Eastern Times*.

Eventually, the desire to reach a broader audience led to the founding in 1995 of The Wisdom Fund, and the setting-up of it's web site at www.twf.org. The site regularly hosts visitors from more than 70 countries.

The War on Islam is based upon the News & Views prepared by me for The Wisdom Fund. As such, while some repetition is inevitable, the individual chapters—which serve as an antidote to the less than objective and/or balanced media coverage of events which helped shape American perspectives of Islam and Muslims, and Muslims' perspectives of America—may be read in any order, and are written to appeal to a wider audience than the typical book on the subjects covered herein.

Hopefully, these glimpses of the war on Islam (and for the non-Muslim, a glimpse of Islam)—which offer perspectives generally missing from major U.S. media—will awaken concerned Americans and Muslims to the tactics used to divide us. Such understanding may move us closer to our goal of justice and peace for all.

For the reader who seldom ventures beyond major media, this book promises a journey through new, and often disturbing, terrain.

Enver Masud
March 2000

"Newsrooms that do not reflect America's diversity
do their readers an injustice.
They fail to tell the stories of its citizens,
they give readers a distorted image of themselves and
they grossly twist the reality of minority groups."

— Dorothy Gilliam
The Washington Post
December 20, 1997

Contents

"Science flourishes on criticism.
Dangerous propaganda crumbles before it."

— Alfred McLung Lee & Elizabeth Bryant Lee
The Fine Art of Propaganda
1939

THE WAR ON ISLAM

March 1, 1991

The Holocaust

January 16, 1991 marks the beginning of the darkest forty-three days in recent American history.

On this day, the United States and its allies, began the systematic destruction of a country whose defense spending was about one percent that of the U.S. In the next forty-three days the guardians of the "civilized world" would kill a hundred thousand men, women, and children, wound a million more, and destroy $200 billion worth of property in the cradle of civilization.

Their cause was "just." They were after the new Hitler. Never mind that until August 1990, this Hitler was their ally in the war with Iran. Never mind that President Saddam Hussein, by no means admired by many of his own people, was not nearly the worst of his breed.

And, of course, oil and the intractable problems at home had nothing to do with it. President George Bush proclaimed a New World Order. Or was it merely old world imperialism? Divide, conquer, plunder, and keep the natives in their place.

The invasion of Kuwait was wrong. Iraq should have settled its dispute with Kuwait peacefully. But was the nature and scale of the U.S. response (sanctioned by a United Nations bullied and bribed into submission) proportionate to the atrocities committed by Iraq?

Having stalemated the United Nations for years, the United States in its newly found zeal, led the western crusade to rid the world of Saddam Hussein.

Never mind that it was silent when Israel bombed Iraq in 1981. Never mind the twenty-three-year occupation by Israel of the West Bank. Never mind all the other atrocities which Amnesty International has reported year after year. Saddam Hussein became the monster that had to be beheaded.

The vast majority in the western world applauded, as they viewed the real life Nintendo game on their television screens. Never mind that lost in the fog of "precision" laser bombing were thousands of innocent men, women and children.

Never mind that the United Nations resolution called only for removing Iraq from Kuwait. While babies in Iraq went without milk, the armchair Rambos, ensconced before their television screens, smelled blood. They howled for going all the way to Baghdad.

They were comforted by an American president who assured them that the United States had no gripe with the Iraqi people. They were only after that new Hitler. Tell that to those Iraqi people who will live with the wounds of war for generations to come.

But a brave minority kept alive the flame of freedom and justice. For upholding the right to free speech, and protesting President Bush's relentless rush to war, they were labeled unpatriotic. This minority did not forget the principles of the founding fathers, and the siren song of freedom that brought their forefathers past the Statue of Liberty.

This minority realized the horrors being committed, and may yet awaken America's conscience, so that freedom and justice for all are the principles which guide us in our dealings with nations and people everywhere.

So while we revel in the euphoria of an unprecedented victory, let us not forget the holocaust in Iraq.

[According to the award winning documentary *Panama Deception*, the U.S. invasion of Panama to capture Gen. Noriega took about ten times as many lives as were taken by Iraq's invasion of Kuwait.]

["Tanks pulling plows moved alongside trenches, firing into the Iraqi soldiers inside the trenches as the plows covered them with great mounds of sand. Thousands were buried, dead, wounded, or alive."—William Blum, *Killing Hope*, p. 334]

October 1, 1991

United Nations of America?

The haste with which the United Nations Security Council passed Resolution 678 authorizing the use of force against Iraq, and its actions since the end of this round of fighting in the Gulf, leave little doubt as to who is setting UN policy and objectives.

The UN actions in the Gulf contrast sharply with UN inaction on other long-standing disputes such as those over Kashmir, Lebanon, and Palestine, which have been allowed to fester despite the passage of UN resolutions. To an unbiased observer it should be obvious that a double standard is at work where the UN and the United States are concerned.

The prostitution of the UN to the wishes of one superpower, endangers the very foundation on which the UN was conceived. It inspires little confidence in less powerful nations when one sees the world's nuclear superpowers, which among them have over forty thousand nuclear warheads, rail sanctimoniously against weaker nations such as Iraq, India, and Pakistan for even attempting to build a single nuclear warhead.

And nothing is said of the State of Israel, imposed upon the Middle East by the colonial powers of the West, which is the major source of instability in the Middle East. Israel's nuclear arsenal is not even acknowledged, while a Muslim nation is humiliated by the U.S. led UN searching for evidence of Iraq's nuclear program.

Of course the U.S. has always had a powerful voice in the UN. However, with the collapse of the Soviet Union the system of checks and balances, without which no organization can function effectively, has also collapsed. The UN Security Council has become little more than an extension of the U.S. Department of State.

That may be good for the U.S. in the short run. But in the long run, the transformation of the UN into a new "United Nations of America" may not serve the needs of any nation.

June 1, 1994

The Third Wave and the New World Order

A new world order is emerging which has little to do with the professed ideology of nations, but is based primarily upon countries' states of technological development.

Writing in *War And Anti-War*, renowned futurists Alvin and Heidi Toffler, define three levels of technological development, the First, Second, and Third Wave, corresponding to countries reaching the heights of the Agricultural Age, the Industrial Age, and the Information Age. The term wave is used because like a wave there occurs a gradual buildup in technological development which reaches a crest, and is followed by another wave.

While many countries have experienced the First and Second Wave, only a few countries like the United States and Japan are at the stage where the Third Wave has begun to be experienced. That is not to say that many other countries have not entered the Information Age. However, these countries are only experiencing the gradual buildup of information technology, but not the crest which marks the wave approaching it's peak. While other countries are building industries, many industries in the U.S. are in decline. Increasingly, wealth in the U.S. is being created in the information technologies and services sector.

Third Wave countries are characterized by organizations which are decentralized, have few layers, are task oriented or matrix instead of hierarchical, are highly dependent on sophisticated information and communications systems in which communications flow not only from top to bottom, but also from bottom to top and sideways. Organizations in the U.S. are going through a re-engineering process and are emerging leaner, more efficient, and more effective. The U.S. armed forces are no exception to this trend.

The relevance of the First, Second, and Third Wave, according to the Tofflers, is that the way nations make wealth parallels the way they make war. The Gulf War marked the first test of the $200 billion U.S. space machine. It was the first major instance where combat forces were deployed, sustained, commanded, and controlled through satellite communications.

Virtually the first shot fired by the U.S. knocked out Iraq's information and communication capabilities. After knocking out Iraq's southern radar defenses, Iraq's electrical systems were crippled with (then secret) bombs that dispersed thousands of carbon filaments to short circuit transmission lines. In essence, the war was over in the first few hours. The importance of information and communications during the Gulf War is underscored by the fact that these systems involved 12 commercial satellites, 118 mobile ground stations, which handled up to 700,000 telephone calls and 152,000 messages per day!

Third Wave capabilities open up entirely new vistas of war making and terrorism. Increasingly, the emphasis in war will be on the acquisition and use of information, the disruption of the enemy's information and communication capabilities, and in disinformation necessary for public support. Terrorists will have new tools at their disposal. Imagine the havoc which would have been created at the World Trade Center if at the height of the Gulf War, instead of a bomb, terrorists were able to disrupt communications with an electromagnetic pulse. The world's financial markets would have been in disarray, and it may have altered the course of the Gulf War. Despite the euphoria that followed the fall of the Iron Curtain, the reasons for war have not changed. Nations make war, as they have throughout history, to acquire resources, to acquire markets, and to acquire allies who will aid in acquiring resources or markets.

Yesterday, historically speaking, the Americas were conquered and native populations decimated to acquire wealth for the Europeans. The British, having nothing the Chinese wanted, forced India, conquered for its spices to grow opium, and forced China to buy the opium. Today, the U.S. and Western Europe with the aid of Egypt, Kuwait, Saudi Arabia, Turkey, and others fight the Gulf War to maintain control of low-priced, Middle-East oil. The historical reasons for war have not changed; only the methods for fighting war, and for numbing the public to the morality of war, have evolved.

Naturally, Third Wave nations will attempt to maintain their superiority both in making wealth and making war. While we hear talk of nuclear nonproliferation and limits on missile capabilities and chemical and biological warfare corresponding to Second Wave technologies, there is much less talk of the nonproliferation of Third Wave war making technologies. Moreover, unlike Second Wave technologies, Third Wave technologies are predominantly dual use. That is they can be used both for war and peaceful purposes. Third Wave countries, while increasing their lead in Third Wave technologies, will increasingly favor the dismantling or dumping of Second Wave war making technologies. They will attempt to dump Second Wave technologies upon First and Second Wave countries, thereby assuring the latter's continued weakness and depletion of wealth, while assuring Third Wave countries' access to First and Second Wave countries' markets and resources.

Second Wave countries may be better off developing or buying more Third Wave weaponry instead of Second Wave weaponry. The example of India's worldwide superiority in Unix may be worth following. India became a world leader in Unix software by essentially skipping the mainframe computer revolution, and moving directly to personal and distributed computing. Can a country entering the industrial age, by selective development, skip the Second Wave, and move toward the Third Wave thereby becoming a world power?

The alliances resulting from the way countries make both wealth and war are creating a New World Order which trisects the world into countries aligned by their having attained First, Second, and Third Wave capabilities. This New World Order is defined more by a nation's technological achievements, and less by its professed ideology.

April 20, 1995

Oklahoma Blast Victims: Innocent Dead, Falsely Accused

The Wisdom Fund, a Washington area nonprofit corporation dedicated to combating misinformation about Islam and Muslims, declared that the tragedy in Oklahoma that killed scores of innocents, now has the potential for criminalizing the entire Muslim community, and undermining their civil rights.

The Oklahoma blast was a heinous act, and must be severely prosecuted. The massacre of innocents, and the devastation of the lives of their loved ones, shall forever remain a tragedy.

Equally craven was the rush to judgment. Within an hour of the horror former Congressman Dave McCurdy was on CBS talking about "very clear evidence of fundamentalist Islamic terrorist groups." In support, he quoted the PBS propaganda piece *Jihad in America* produced by the perennial Muslim-baiter Steven Emerson. The media, including CNN, joined in the fray.

Responsible Federal law enforcement officials were, however, more circumspect. They were cited on the front page of the *New York Times* of April 20 as stating that they "had no suspect," and that investigators "did not know whether the bombers were domestic or international terrorists."

Meanwhile, the damage has been done to innocent Oklahomans including the Oklahoma Muslim community, which has been doubly terrorized by the bomb blast and by false accusations of complicity in the crime. The object appears to be to put Muslims outside the pale of mainstream America as was once done to the Japanese. This has occurred only because Muslims, unlike others, have no effective lobby and are seen as easy targets.

We are reminded of the wise words of another: "a society is judged by how well it protects the rights of the least powerful." There are two victims of the Oklahoma tragedy: the innocent dead, and the falsely accused.

April 23, 1995

Oklahoma City Blast: Media Coverage Biased

"Have you heard of the Michigan Militia?" was the question we asked at the Catholic-Muslim Dialogue, January 12, 1995, sponsored by the Secretariat for Ecumenical and Interreligious Affairs, National Conference of Catholic Bishops in Washington, D.C. No one had heard of this radical group, but all were aware of "Islamic terrorists."

Media bias is so evident. Just examine stories in which Muslims are involved, and those in which Christians or Jews are involved. In the former you will see the person's faith noted, in the latter you generally won't.

Media coverage of Islam and Muslims would fail Journalism 101. Journalists are trained to report the who, what, when, where, why, and how of stories. The "who" in stories of Christians and Jews is a human being, often described by friends, family, teachers, neighbors, if relevant to the story. Very seldom is their religion mentioned. In the case of Muslims, religion is invariably mentioned, and it is about the only thing mentioned of this "other" being. In the case of Christians and Jews, there is usually much discussion of "why" the person did what he or she did. In the case of Muslims, all the reader is told is that the person was a militant, or extremist, or fundamentalist, as if that were sufficient explanation.

The media appear to have excruciating difficulty writing about Muslims without mentioning their religion. In "Through the Minefield of Political Islam," *Washington Post*, March 31, 1995, Stephen S. Rosenfeld describes his difficulties in writing about Muslims and Islam. He has no such difficulty in writing about other faiths. Why not write about Muslims and Islam, the same way in which one writes about Christians and Christianity?

Following the capture of an alleged Oklahoma City bomber, the *Washington Post*, April 22, 1995, carried a story titled "Muslim's Burden of Blame Lifts" by Laurie Goodstein and Marylou Tousignant. If the burden has been lifted from Muslims, on whom does it fall? On Christians? Of course not. The point is the burden should never have been placed on Muslims. While the story itself may be accurate, the need for such a story should never have arisen.

Will the media behave more responsibly in the future? Will Muslims, to paraphrase the lead in the movie *Network*, wake up and say, "We're mad as hell, we're not going to take it anymore," and take the media to task? Only time will tell.

April 28, 1995

Jihad Against Islam

A fact here, a fact there, conclusions out of nowhere, and pretty soon you have an Islamic conspiracy to subjugate the United States and terrorize the world. In the recent PBS documentary *Jihad in America,* producer Steven Emerson, in his struggle to piece together a story, has set forth on his own jihad against Islam and Muslims.

Emerson begins with scenes of the World Trade Center bombing, and the arguable conclusion that the ultimate goal of Muslim extremists is to establish an Islamic empire. The fact that the so-called extremists are waging a struggle to recover their lands from which they were forcibly evicted, or struggling for freedom from foreign domination, a fundamental ideal subscribed to by our founding fathers, is not mentioned.

After a perfunctory disclaimer that Islam or Muslims are not the issue in *Jihad in America,* which aired on PBS on November 21, 1994, Emerson and the experts interviewed mention Islam or Muslim about once a minute for the next fifteen minutes (we stopped counting after that). Contrast this with coverage of Christian or Jewish wrongdoing where the religion of the criminal, the militant, or extremist is seldom mentioned.

We are told "most Americans understand very little about Islam." Emerson, however, only adds to the misunderstanding. We are not told that Islam is the religion based on God's message conveyed by a line of prophets including Abraham, Moses, Jesus, and Muhammad. We are also not told that Islam recognizes Muslims, Jews, and Christians as "People of the Book."

Where Islam unites Muslims, Jews, and Christians, Emerson struggles to divide. Jihad, the subject of the "documentary," is not even defined. We are not told that jihad has many definitions, that in general it means struggle, and that the highest form of jihad is the struggle against self.

Emerson then pieces together film clips from diverse sources, and interviews with a handful of "experts." From this meager "evidence" he takes a gigantic leap to the conclusion that there is an Islamic conspiracy to rule the world. The documentary is filled with half truths, misstatements, and questionable conclusions. Some examples follow.

Afghanistan's freedom fighters, which were supported by the U.S. in their fight to expel the Soviet invasion, are portrayed as Islamic rebels "dedicated to spreading jihad." Having expelled the Soviets, these freedom fighters talk of spreading their jihad (struggle) to aid neighboring countries dominated by other foreign powers. Surely "life, liberty, and the pursuit of happiness" is not for the U.S. alone.

Yes, Islam is used to rally the freedom fighters, but it is hardly a call to an armed war to spread Islam around the world. We talk of our War on Poverty; War on Drugs. President Reagan spoke of a "Crusade Against Drugs." Can Emerson not understand the hyperbole in the language of others?

Emerson jumps from the Ayatollah Khomeini led revolution in Iran to the assassination of President Sadat. The viewer is not told that it was the Shah of Iran's brutal suppression of his people, or of foreign meddling and domination in the Middle East that has caused so much suffering. Instead, selected events are tied together to draw us to Emerson's conclusion of a grand Islamic conspiracy.

Emerson sees danger lurking everywhere. The stationery of the Alkifah Refugee Center in Peshawar, Pakistan (supported by the U.S.), which in translation reads "Office of Services to the Holy Warriors," is a "fact" pointing to a grand Islamic conspiracy. Emerson and the late Senator McCarthy, who saw communists everywhere, would have found a lot in common.

Abdullah Azzam, an Afghan freedom fighter, is given prominence in spreading jihad against Jews, Christians, and moderate Muslims. Azzam may be talking of an armed war or a struggle to overcome foreign domination in the Middle East. But Azzam's speaking before groups in the U.S. does not prove a conspiracy to wage an Islamic war on the U.S.

Was Azzam the sole speaker at these meetings? Who else spoke, what was said, what action was taken, we are not told. Azzam speaks of the Soviets who invaded Afghanistan as the "enemy of Allah." Is this a call to Islamic war as Emerson portrays it, or merely Azzam's way of portraying the Soviet invaders, and their surrogates, so as to rally Afghan Muslims to drive out the Soviets? Emerson is drawn unquestionably to his conclusion of an Islamic jihad against the world.

We're shown a map of the Middle East and North Africa, and told that "Islamic holy warriors began launching attacks against Israel, Egypt, and Algeria." Who controls these attacks, what is the motive? We are not told. But Emerson has no doubts that they are all connected in a grand Islamic conspiracy.

From the Middle East and North Africa Emerson jumps to Azzam's fund raising efforts in the U.S., and branches of the Alkifah Refugee Center at several U.S. locations, as evidence of jihad in America. Is fund raising by the Irish in America who support the IRA, the Jews who support the extremists in Israel, or the fiery speeches of Louis Farrakhan, evidence of a conspiracy against America?

Target shooting practice by unidentified individuals is portrayed by Emerson as evidence of Muslims training for holy war. What is their connection with specific acts of violence? How are they connected in some grand Islamic conspiracy? Emerson tells us that they are, but for all we know the target shooters may only be members of the National Rifle Association pursuing their hobby.

In short, Emerson has taken a real act of terror, the bombing of the World Trade Center, and isolated events and persons from Pakistan to the U.S. and woven them with invisible threads into a grand Islamic conspiracy against the world. We know terrorists exist within many countries and communities. We also know one man's terrorist may be another's freedom fighter. Emerson fails to show us the threads which weave these diverse Muslims into a jihad against America.

In a nation of immigrants faced with rising tensions among communities, racial divisions, and frustration with immigration, Emerson uses a broad brush to denigrate Islam and Muslims. He misses the opportunity to present issues fairly, to create understanding, and possibly lead to a just resolution of legitimate grievances. *Jihad in America* is not a documentary. It is a propaganda film like those used to demonize Jews in the days of Hitler.

August 5, 1995

O.J. and Sheikh Rahman—Double Standards of Justice

Our system of justice is supposed to lean in the direction of freeing the potentially guilty, rather than incarcerating the potentially innocent. When we examine the cases against of Mr. O. J. Simpson and Sheikh Abdel Rahman, we find that the defendant against whom there was the least evidence will be incarcerated.

We do not know whether Mr. Simpson committed the murders of which he stands accused. Based upon media reports we do know, however, that except for Mr. Mark Fuhrman, the evidence and witnesses against Mr. Simpson were more credible than the evidence and witnesses against Sheikh Rahman.

The *New York Times* reported that the evidence that Sheikh Rahman even knew of the plan to bomb the World Trade Center, and other buildings in New York, is scant. The government's primary witness against Sheikh Rahman is an FBI informant, Mr. Emad Salem, who confessed to lying under oath in a previous trial. Six months before the World Trade Center bombing, the FBI terminated Mr. Salem after he failed several lie detector tests. Following the bombing Mr. Salem was rehired for a fee of over $1 million.

The double standards of our system of "justice," and the moral bankruptcy of the "experts" is exposed. Most media and expert analyses is focussed upon the Simpson case, and almost none on the Sheikh Rahman case. If our system is supposed to lean toward freeing the potentially guilty, rather than incarcerating the potentially innocent, the focus of analyses should be on the Sheikh Rahman case where the government used an ancient law regarding seditious conspiracy to silence an unpopular critic.

For Muslims, who were unjustly accused in the aftermath of the Oklahoma City bombing, the Sheikh Rahman case is further evidence of the cold war with Islam which began with the demise of the Soviet Union. Until Muslims are better organized, the future holds more of the same for Muslims in America.

August 9, 1995

"The Truth About Islam" Presented to Cardinal Arinze

Cardinal Arinze, at a landmark dialogue with Muslim leaders, was presented "The Truth About Islam," a 600 word introduction to Islam, on behalf of the Wisdom Fund.

The occasion was a dialogue on Muslim-Christian relations in the world today, hosted by the National Conference of Catholic Bishops and Catholic Relief Services, U.S. Catholic Conference, at the CRS headquarters in Baltimore, Maryland. Muslim leaders from across the U.S. were invited to a roundtable dialogue with H.E. Francis Cardinal Arinze, President, Pontifical Council for Inter-Religious Dialogue at the Holy See.

Cardinal Arinze spoke of the need to "look beyond the past," and to "begin the process of healing memory." Quoting Prophet Muhammad, "No man is a true believer unless he desires for his brother that which he desires for himself," Cardinal Arinze underscored the need to build upon the shared values of Islam and Christianity which bind over one half of the world's population. Cardinal William H. Keeler of the Archdiocese of Baltimore called media reporting on Islam "cynical and sensational."

Mowahid Shah, attorney at law and editor of *Eastern Times*, speaking on behalf of Muslims, urged religious leaders to speak out forcefully against the false stigmatizing of Islam and Muslims. "There were two victims of the Oklahoma City bombing—the innocent dead and the falsely accused," said Shah. Prof. Esposito, director of Georegetown University Center for Muslim and Christian Understanding, stressed the need to examine media reporting in the wake of the Oklahoma bombing.

The text of the presentation to Cardinal Arinze includes sayings of Prophet Muhammad, and is contained in the Appendix. "The Truth About Islam" is the centerpiece of the Wisdom Fund's advertising campaign to inform Americans of the history and values shared by Islam and Christianity.

August 22, 1995

Muslim Children Forcibly Converted to Christianity

An ABC 20/20 program which aired Friday, August 18, 10:00 PM EST, depicts the plight of a Muslim family, Sadri and Sebhat Krasniqi, who had two children snatched from their custody because, according to a Texas judge, they would be better off in a Christian home.

The assumption that the children would be better off in a Christian home was clearly articulated by the presiding judge who told 20/20 that a Christian home would provide greater stability. The children's father was subsequently acquitted of the charges, which led to the custody battle, of sexually abusing his four-year-old daughter. Furthermore, the Texas Department of Child Protective Services violated its own guidelines requiring it "to seek placement of the children with the closest religious and ethnic match."

The Muslim children, now living in a Christian home, have been forced to convert to Christianity, and to eat pork, which under Muslim dietary laws (similar to Jewish dietary laws) is strictly forbidden. The Krasniqi's, because of mounting legal bills, have had to sell the four restaurants the immigrant family had acquired in their pursuit of the American dream.

The judge's decision, if allowed to stand, is an ugly stain on our democratic ideals, and casts serious doubts on the constitutional rights of minorities and Muslims in America.

September 14, 1995

Peace Prize Awakens Ghosts of Nazi Germany

The award of Germany's most prestigious cultural prize to Annemarie Schimmel, 73, a Harvard professor for over 20 years, has awakened the ghosts of Nazi Germany.

Prof. Schimmel, one of the world's leading experts on Islamic mysticism, will next month be presented The Peace Prize of the German

Book Trade. She will join a line of luminaries which include Albert Schweitzer, Vaclav Havel, Martin Buber, and George Kennan.

The announced award has resulted in a storm of protests from about 220 writers, 100 publishing houses, and several members of parliament who accuse Prof. Schimmel of being too sympathetic to Islamic fundamentalism. The protestors, including novelist Gunter Grass and philosopher Jurgen Habermas say, "This German Orientalist is a welcome guest in totalitarian Islamic states like Iran, but in her entire work there is not a single reference to human rights violations in these countries."

These protests are reminiscent of Nazi Germany and other totalitarian regimes. What is more worrisome is the fact that this climate of xenophobic intolerance has spilled over into the upper crust, and is no longer confined to the less educated, the working class, or the unemployed. Professor Schimmel is being persecuted for her enlightened perspective on Islam.

Prof. Schimmel's works are aimed at providing a better understanding of the Islamic world and the lives of Muslims. She provides an intellectually valid counterpoint to the generally negative portrayal of Islam and Muslims in mainstream U.S. media.

Dr. Ayub Ommaya, a Director of The Wisdom Fund, and very familiar with Prof. Schimmel's works says, "The charges against her are baseless and irrelevant. Prof. Schimmel is a spiritual person who writes about Islam and the culture of Muslims. Like Mother Theresa, Prof. Schimmel is apolitical, and oblivious of the politics of countries she visits." Prof. Schimmel, now retired from Harvard, is living among a Sufi community in the Sind province of Pakistan.

Former peace prize winner George Kennan, however, turned out to be a closet hawk. Policy Planning Study 23, written by Mr. Kennan for the U.S. State Department in 1948 says in part: "...we have about 50% of the world's wealth, but only 6.3% of its population...Our real task in the coming period is to devise a pattern of relationships which will permit us to maintain this position of disparity...To do so, we will have to dispense with all sentimentality...We should cease to talk about vague and...unreal objectives such as human rights, the raising of living standards, and democratization." This was, of course, a top secret document at the time Kennan was awarded The Peace Prize of the German Book Trade.

Thus far the selection committee has remained steadfast saying, "Much of the material we have received encourages us to stand by our decision." Those who believe in academic freedom must speak out against this brazen attack by the vigilantes of political correctness. If we don't learn from the lessons of the past, we are doomed to revisit it.

October 12, 1995

Pope's Vision Strikes Chord among Muslims

Speaking before the United Nations General Assembly, Pope John Paul II's vision of freedom struck a sympathetic chord among Muslims in America.

Pope John Paul said freedom is "fulfilled in man's quest for truth. Detached from the truth about the human person, freedom deteriorates into license into the lives of individuals." The Pope spoke out against "the arrogance of power," and "Utilitarianism, the doctrine which defines morality not in terms of what is good but of what is advantageous. The subjugation, for example, of a smaller or weaker nation is claimed to be a good thing solely because it corresponds to the national interest."

The Pope's message at the UN was reinforced in Baltimore, MD, the site of the first Catholic church in America. The Pope spoke of justice and peace—tenets central to Islam. The Baltimore event was covered by the Faith & Values Channel, broadcast nationwide, which invited representatives of the Christian, Jewish, and Muslim community to comment upon the Papal parade live from their studios in New York. The invitees included Jim Hartz, former anchor of the NBC Today Show; Mr. A. J. Cernera president of Sacred Heart University, Rabbi Bemporad, director Jewish Christian Relations, and Father O'Keefe; and Mowahid Shah, editor *Eastern Times*, attorney-at-law, and an advisor at The Wisdom Fund.

Shah, speaking on the Faith & Values Channel, emphasized Islam's concepts of justice which promote "empathy for the needy, and identification with the have-nots." Shah praised the Pope's firm stance on principles rather than bending to current popular positions. "The Pope's message of freedom and justice for all," said Shah, "is central to Islam, which recognizes Jews and Christians as people of the Book, and is rooted in the monotheistic message of Abraham, later prophets, and completed by the Prophet Muhammad. The symmetry between the Catholic and Muslim faiths," said Shah, "was also reflected in the positions taken by the Vatican and Muslim organizations during the World Population Conference earlier this year in Cairo, Egypt."

November 22, 1995

Bosnia "Peace" Treaty Rings Hollow, Future Bleak

The Bosnia peace agreement, brokered in private marathon sessions by the Clinton administration, raises many more questions than it answers. One thing, however, is certain: the clarion call "never again" rings hollow, and in effect aggression pays.

If the pact seems to be working it would be a godsend for President Clinton in his second term election bid. But if American peacekeeping forces in Bosnia suffer heavy casualties it could be his political demise. The big domestic question is whether the Republican-controlled Congress will authorize, and even more importantly, finance, the sending of some 20,000 American troops under NATO command to the Balkans. Senator Bob Dole, the leading contender for the Republican presidential nomination, has instead repeatedly called for the lifting of the arms embargo against the Bosnians.

Exhausted now, the parties to the brutal war in Bosnia, mercifully, have agreed to stop the killing. But the future looks bleak for the Bosnian Muslims.

Why did the U.S.-led West deny the Bosnians that most basic of human rights: the right to self-defense? What will the peace pact achieve that could not have been realized without the sacrifice of tens of thousands of Bosnian Muslim Serbs? Had President Bush stood firm, the

Orthodox Christian Serbs could have been stopped dead in their tracks. But there was to be no "line in the sand" for the Serbs. Mr. Bush had an election coming, the euphoria over the Gulf War was wearing thin, and the U.S. had no vital interests, like oil, in far-off Bosnia.

Today, a number of factors have come together. In recent months, the Roman Catholic Croats and Bosnian Muslim Serbs have recaptured large parts of their territories from the Christian Serbs. This exploded Washington's nonintervention scenario that repulsing the aggressor Christian Serbs could involve the U.S. in an open-ended Vietnam-type war. The United Nation's dismal peacekeeping failure, the differences between NATO allies and the Atlantic Alliance's exposure as "a paper tiger," along with reports of large scale Christian Serb war crimes forced the Clinton administration to say "enough is enough" and get NATO air power to knock out Christian Serb radar systems and weapons. Meanwhile, the international sanctions against Belgrade were hurting Serbia. President Slobodan Milosevic, now uncertain of support from the ailing Russian President Yeltsin, was forced to accept the Clinton peace accord.

But for Bosnia itself the future looks grim. Major issues remain unresolved. How long will U.S. troops be in Bosnia to keep the peace? If fighting breaks out again, will the Bosnian government have access to military supplies. Will refugees return to their properties or receive compensation and from whom? Will those indicted for war crimes, like the Bosnian Serb leader Radovan Karadzic, be handed over for trial by the International War Crimes Tribunal at The Hague. Will those whose friends and families have fought and died in the holocaust learn to live again in peace?

And will Bosnia be partitioned, like the Middle East, India, and other countries were partitioned by foreign powers. The aftereffects of those actions are felt keenly by the citizens of those countries to this day. Is Bosnia's misery over? No. Will Bosnia even continue to exist as agreed to in the treaty? Will the Muslims ultimately be left with only a city/state: Sarajevo?

November 23, 1995

Toledo Mosque: Uplifting Sight, Outstanding Community

Driving North on Interstate 75, about an hour South of Detroit, Michigan, one's eyes are drawn to the gleaming white dome and minarets of a mosque. As one gets nearer one sees a magnificent white structure which a sign proclaims is the Islamic Center of Greater Toledo.

The weary traveler, having passed miles of cookie-cutter Americana, cannot but feel his spirits soar at this uplifting sight. Built on forty-eight acres of land in 1983, the mosque and surrounding buildings today cover 40,000 square feet. The sixty-foot dome is flanked by two 135-foot minarets. The octagonal prayer room can accommodate 1000 people, there is a 500 seat sermon hall, classroom, offices, a medical clinic, a huge dining room, and a large commercial kitchen. There are plans to add two wings: one for a full-time school, and the other for a home for the elderly. Tours are conducted regularly.

Having been invited to speak at the 12th anniversary celebrations of the Islamic Center, it was the outstanding Muslim community I found there which most endeared me to that place. The subject of the seminar was Islam and Media. The speakers included Prof. William Green, dean of undergraduate studies at the University of Rochester; Prof. Jack Shaheen, nationally known commentator and writer, Sr. Sharifa Alkhateeb of the Muslim Women's Georgetown Study Project, Mr. Richard Paton, an editor at *The Blade*, and the author, representing The Wisdom Fund.

The Muslim, Christian, and Jewish speakers agreed that media coverage of Islam and Muslims was largely negative. All, except Mr. Paton, agreed on the need to get more Muslims into the media. Mr. Paton's reservations about this suggestion are, perhaps, understandable since *The Blade* appears to be an exception and frequently carries profiles of Muslims and articles from Dr. S. Amjad Hussain, a regular contributor to *The Blade* and President of the Islamic Center.

The audience for the seminar included Muslim's from many professions, Christians, and at least one Hindu. The Muslim women were not restrained by the strict separation common to some Muslim communities. In fact, the prayer room has only a three foot divider separating the men from women. The seminar and Anniversary Dinner were covered by local media, the mayor attended, and congratulations from George V. Voinovich, Governor of Ohio and the Greater Toledo community were contained in a 30-page program handed out at dinner. Dr. Saleh Jabrin, a major force behind the building of the mosque, was honored by having a new wing dedicated in his name.

Having attended functions at other Muslim centers, I was struck with how well everything was managed. Events were on time, children well behaved, and everything worked smoothly. In the heartland of the United States, the Muslim community of Greater Toledo, the management of the Islamic Center, and the charming and progressive Imam A. M. Khattab have set a standard for enlightened Muslims in America.

January 26, 1996

Why the West Fears Islam

When one examines the West's fear of Islam, and tries to relate it to the reasons usually given—Muslim fundamentalism, militancy, radicalism, terrorism, totalitarianism—it is difficult, if not impossible, to justify this fear on the basis of the reasons usually given. One has to believe, however, given all the facts and expertise available to the West, that the fear has to be rational. What is this fear that causes enemies of the Muslim world to play subtly on the theme of the Crusades in order to demonize Islam and Muslims? Let us first examine what it is not, before we draw our conclusion as to the real reason why the West fears Islam.

The fear of Islamic fundamentalism, militancy, radicalism, terrorism, totalitarianism, and the West's discovery of the "rogue states," appeared quite conveniently with the fall of the Berlin Wall and the disintegration of the Soviet Union. Former Defense Secretary McNamara, in his 1989 testimony before the Senate Budget Committee, said U.S. defense spending could safely be cut in half. It became clear that the U.S. had to either undergo massive shifts in spending, a painful and unwelcome prospect for the defense establishment, or find new justification for continuing high levels of military expenditures. To provide this justification, the Pentagon manufactured the threat of "rogue states and nuclear outlaws." The Gulf War was a contrived opportunity to sell this justification to the American people, to protect oil company profits, and to control the flow of oil to Europe and Japan which need it much more than does the U.S.

The International Institute for Strategic Studies calculates that the $262 billion U.S. defense budget accounts for about 37 percent of global military expenditures. Russia, Japan, and China will spend about $80 billion, $42 billion, and $7 billion respectively. The six "rogue states"—Cuba, Iran, Iraq, Libya, Syria, North Korea—have a combined annual military budget of $15 billion. The U.S. budget for covert operations (U.S. terrorism?) alone is double this amount. Given the paltry defense expenditures of all the "rogue states" combined, even after correcting for differences in costs, one has to believe that the "rogue states" are no match, militarily, for the West.

And, leaving aside the morality of U.S. covert operations which invite retaliation, Muslim terrorists should not be a major fear. Far more acts of terrorism and violent crime in the U.S., according to government statistics, are committed by non-Muslims than Muslims. And if Muslims do pose a terrorist threat to the U.S., one hears little discussion of what it is that the terrorists want. Perhaps, all they want is for the West to stop interfering in their countries, in ways that we would never tolerate in the U.S.

Islamic totalitarianism, an oxymoron to anyone with even a rudimentary knowledge of Islam, should not be a Western concern. A Muslim ruler may be totalitarian, but then her rule would not be Islamic. Furthermore, the Western record on supporting totalitarian Muslim regimes—Iran under the Shah, Iraq before the Gulf War—and doing business with nondemocratic regimes—China, Kuwait, Saudi Arabia—speaks for itself.

As for fundamentalism, Islam has no parallel to the U.S. Protestant Christian movement which opposed modern scientific theory, and which coined the term in 1920 to designate those "doing battle royal for the fundamentals." Rather Islam has, from its birth, stressed the use of reason and logic.

Islamic law is based upon the Quran, examples and sayings of Prophet Muhammad, analogical deduction, consensus among the learned, and individual reasoning. According to Muhammad Asad (*The Message of the Quran*) when the Prophet's contemporaries heard the words islam and muslim, they understood them as denoting man's "self-surrender to God" and "one who surrenders himself to God," without limiting himself to any specific community or denomination, eg. in the Quran, 3:67, where Abraham is spoken of as having "surrendered himself unto God" (kana musliman), or in 3:52 where the disciples of Jesus say, "Bear thou witness that we have surrendered ourselves unto God (bianna musliman)." In Arabic, this original meaning has remained unimpaired.

Absent a generally accepted definition, the label Islamic fundamentalism serves only to obscure issues, rather than to resolve them. Meanwhile, the Christian Coalition, and the Zionists and their biblical claim to Palestine appear fundamentalist to many, yet both are courted by U.S. politicians, and not viewed as a threat.

One can go on eliminating Western arguments against Islam and Muslims. Eventually, one has to ask, what then is the source of the West's fear of Islam and Muslims?

The late Marshall G. S. Hodgson, in *Rethinking World History*, states: "[Islam's] conscious hopes for a godly world order represent one of the most remarkable undertakings in world history and because its less self-conscious general cultural heritage is laden with human values." Muslims see the West beset with broken families, violent crime, and drugs. They see a society divided by race, religion, and huge disparities in income. They long for a peaceful life in which they may provide for the basic needs of their families, and enjoy the respect due to all mankind regardless of their race, religion, position, or wealth.

These Muslims see their goals for a more just and compassionate society thwarted by a corrupt Muslim elite who pursue wealth and power regardless of the cost to their fellow human beings. They see these elites, who govern not by consensus as Islam prescribes, permitting outside powers to exploit their country while they derive few benefits, and find themselves subordinated by Western influences driving them down the troubled road taken by the West. They see few opportunities to earn a living because most opportunities are withheld for the elites and their sycophants. And they see these elites remaining silent when their faith, which offers solutions to the many social problems that plague the West, is denigrated in the propaganda which serves to maintain these elites.

The Muslim elites' allies are the defense establishment and the neoimperialists. Islam's mandate for justice and compassion opposes the primary objective of these neoimperialists who seek to follow policies outlined in 1948 by "the leading dove and peace prize winner," Mr. George Kennan, for the U.S. Department of State. In the top secret Policy Planning Study 23, Mr. Kennan stated in part: "...we have about 50% of the world's wealth, but only 6.3% of its population...Our real task in the coming period is to devise a pattern of relationships which will permit us to maintain this position of disparity...To do so, we will have to dispense with all sentimentality...We should cease to talk about vague and...unreal objectives such as human rights, the raising of living standards, and democratization."

To avoid exposure, these neoimperialists and their allies in the U.S. defense establishment, spurred by the enemy within, divert attention by demonizing Islam and Muslims, thereby fanning the fires of bigotry and raising unrealistic fears among the people of the West.

March 9, 1996

Danger of Islam Self-Evident

From the Khomeini-led revolution in Iran to Saddam Hussein's invasion of Kuwait to the bombing of the World Trade Center, the American people have been subjected to relentless anti-Muslim indoctrination. It is imbibed with their mother's milk, stereotyped in their movies, spelled out in fifteen-second soundbites on television. Their daily paper offers them headlines that tell them all they need to know. Politicians and presidents sanctimoniously thrive on it.

The fiercely-held conviction inevitably produced by this insidious assault upon the intellect is that a great damnation has been unleashed upon the world, possibly by the devil himself, but in the form of people—

people not motivated by the same needs, fears, emotions, and personal morality that govern others of the species, but people engaged in an extremely clever, monolithic, international conspiracy dedicated to taking over the world and enslaving it, for reasons not always clear perhaps, but evil needs no motivation save evil itself.

Moreover, any appearance or claim by these people to be rational human beings seeking a better kind of world or society is a sham, a cover-up to delude others, and proof only of their cleverness. The recent bombings which have taken place in Israel are forever proof of the bankruptcy of virtue and the evil intentions of these people in whichever country they may be found, under whatever name they may call themselves. Most importantly, the only choice open to anyone in the United States is between the *American way of life* and *Islam's way of life*—that nothing lies between or beyond these two ways of viewing the world.

This is how it looks to the simple folk of America. One finds that media pundits and establishment experts, when probed slightly beneath the surface of their academic language, see it exactly the same way. To the mind carefully brought to adulthood in the United States, the danger of Islam is self-evident; as self-evident as the flatness of the world once was to an earlier mind.

[Islam having replaced communism as the "Evil Empire," we paraphrased this commentary on communism from William Blum, *Killing Hope: US Military and CIA Interventions Since World War II*, with his permission.]

March 22, 1996

Sacrificing Africans, Muslims to Bring Nile Water to Israel

Are the Sudanese people about to be placed on the sacrificial altar of the Western powers in order to bring water to their progeny—the state of Israel? Are U.S. citizens and Europeans about to be suckered into a "peace-making mission" in Sudan?

It is no secret that Israel is thirsting for new supplies of water. Ever since its birth it has met its water requirements by denying water to the native Palestinians. This may change as the Israeli-PLO "peace process" is played out. And even if current discriminatory water-sharing arrangements continue, Israel is going to need more water to meet its increasing demand. So how does Sudan enter into the picture?

I first heard of secret studies to bring the Nile's water to Israel from a Kenyan hydrological expert in Tanzania who declined to be quoted for fear of reprisals. The Nile, of course, runs through Sudan and Egypt. And while Egypt may be persuaded to surrender its water to Israel, the Sudanese mainly Muslim regime presents a bigger obstacle.

Being a professional engineer and international consultant, when I first heard of it, the proposal seemed rather farfetched. However, recent testimony prepared for the U.S. House of Representatives Committee on International Relations by Ms. Muriel Mirak of the Schiller Institute in Washington, D.C. caused me to reconsider.

Ms. Mirak states that the leading witnesses testifying to alleged white slavery in Sudan "are acting as agents of a foreign power," and "are engaged in witting fraud on the Congress." She further states that the policies being promoted by Christian Solidarity International, allegedly "a vehicle of the intelligence services of Great Britain...if implemented, would unleash genocidal war across the entire region of eastern Africa."

I am reminded of the October 10, 1990 testimony of "Nayirah" who testified that she had watched infants being taken from incubators in a Kuwait City hospital, and that the Iraqi soldiers "left the babies on the cold floor to die." As we now know "Nayirah" was none other than the daughter of the Kuwaiti ambassador in Washington, and that the public relations firm of Hill and Knowlton had staged the event to help former President Bush justify U.S. intervention in Kuwait.

We also know that the current regime in Sudan is considered hostile to U.S. interests, and that the U.S. has for half a century uncritically supported the state of Israel. While we admit there are some missing pieces, here's how we see the scenario, if left unchallenged, will be played out.

The U.S. public is persuaded of human rights abuses in Sudan. The U.S.-led and Great Britain-backed UN passes the needed resolutions. Sudan is subjected to an embargo. When this fails the U.S. and European powers intervene in Sudan, unleashing civil war across eastern Africa. The Sudanese regime is either toppled and replaced with one subservient to the West, or sufficiently humbled to agree to western demands to let Israel have the Nile water. U.S. taxpayers then donate some more billions of dollars to Israel.

Of course, if in the meantime several thousand Africans, Muslims, and possibly Americans are killed so what? We know that Africans don't have the same high regard for human life that we do. Didn't the U.S. Supreme Court once state that African Americans were merely property—not human beings? And those Muslims should welcome the opportunity for "jihad" and martyrdom which would send them straight to heaven. And our boys will have died defending American values.

If all this comes to pass, we can count on our media to give it the proper spin so that we can feel good about going to the aid of yet another third world nation that cannot quite take care of itself. And the U.S. Congress and our President can continue to deny the American people the peace dividend that was to have come from the end of the cold war with the former U.S.S.R.

March 26, 1996

Libya: Who's Terrorizing Whom

Today, the *Washington Post* reported unrest in Libya which the Libyans believe is led by a Col. Khalifa Haftar based in the U.S., and on May 17, 1991 the *Washington Times* reported that three hundred and fifty Libyans would arrive soon in the United States.

It turns out that the Libyans who arrived in the U.S. in 1991 were not the Libyan President Ghaddafi's terrorists. They were our folks, trained by our CIA. These terrorists, which our government (ever mindful of our sensitivities) prefers to call guerillas, were trained by our CIA to topple President Ghaddafi. Last December 1990, when a new government less sympathetic to our mission was formed in Chad, we tried to find another home for our folks. It seemed that no one wanted our recruits, and so they were flown to the United States from Kenya where they were being temporarily housed. Col. Haftar was part of this group.

Col. Haftar is now reported to be the leader of a contra-style group based in the U.S. called the Libyan National Army. This group is supported by the U.S., and has been given training facilities in the U.S. It's a good presumption that Col. Haftar's group operates in Libya with the blessings of our government.

The question is, "Is Libya terrorizing the U.S., or is the U.S. terrorizing Libya?" Imagine the media frenzy if the situation were reversed.

["A top-secret report linking MI6 with a failed attempt to assassinate Colonel Gadaffi appeared on an American internet site yesterday."—Nicholas Rufford, "Revealed: Cook Misled Public over Libya Plot," *Sunday Times*, February 13, 2000]

March 29, 1996

Propaganda Merchants Posing as Terrorism Experts

At a seminar on terrorism, held yesterday at the prestigious Center for Strategic and International Studies of George Washington University, all it took was two simple questions to expose experts on terrorism for what they are—merchants of anti-Islamic propaganda. The seminar panel included the head of the CSIS terrorism project, a Voice of America spokesman, former officials of the U.S. Department of State, and others from various think tanks.

The experts delivered the usual anti-Islamic propaganda: mosques posing as fronts for terrorists groups; the threat of the rogue states of Iran, Iraq, Libya, Sudan, Syria, and the proliferation of weapons of mass destruction. When finally permitted to speak, we asked, "Why is there no one on the panel with an opposing point of view, and why would these countries want to terrorize the United States?"

In all my years managing research programs and projects for the U.S. government and around the world, I cannot recall a single issue as broad as terrorism on which experts did not have opposing views. Only by sifting through opposing views can one hope to arrive at the truth. And what motive do Iran, Iraq, Libya, Sudan, Syria have to terrorize the

U.S.? Given that the $262 billion U.S. defense budget accounts for about 37 percent of global military expenditures, while the six rogue states—Cuba, Iran, Iraq, Libya, Syria, North Korea—have a combined annual military budget of $15 billion, what do these 'rogue' states hope to gain?

The panel on terrorism had no answer. They did, however, ask who we would recommend for future panels. We gave three names: William Blum—former employee of the U.S. Department of State; Noam Chomsky—youngest tenured professor at MIT; Howard Zinn—professor at Boston University. All are of Jewish origin.

April 25, 1996

Gunning for Libya: The Holocaust Continues

At a Defense Department briefing on April 23 a senior defense official stated that the United States would not exclude the use of nuclear weapons to destroy Libya's chemical plant at Tarhunah. This plant, said the official, "is not in the interest of peace, not in the interest of stability, and not in the interest of world order."

Libya was blamed in the 1970s and '80s, writes William Blum in *Killing Hope*, for supporting "a wide array of radical/insurgent/terrorist organizations...in various parts of the Middle East, Africa, and Asia; as well as the IRA and Basque and Corsican separatists in Europe...the list is without end." "It is the notion," writes Bill Schaap in *Covert Action Information Bulletin*, No. 30, "that the Libyan leader, Col. Muammar Qaddafi, is responsible for every act of terrorism in the world."

Not too long ago native American savages served the same purpose. The rogue states have replaced native American savages as the new all purpose villains.

"Our evidence is direct, it is precise, it is irrefutable," announced U.S. President Reagan in explaining the American bombing attack on Libya of April 14, 1986 in retaliation for the alleged Libyan bombing nine days earlier of a West Berlin nightclub frequented by U.S. servicemen. The German government, however, remained critical and skeptical of the American position linking Libya to the bombing. Five months after the December 21, 1988 explosion of Pan Am flight 103 over Lockerbie, Scotland, the U.S. State Department announced that the CIA was confident that the villains were members of the Popular Front for the Liberation of Palestine led by Ahmed Jibril based in Syria. But when Syria allied with the U.S. in the Gulf War the blame was shifted to Libya.

Conveniently ignored is U.S. bombing of innocent civilians in Libya, including Col. Qaddafi's young daughter, the calculated devastation of Iraq during the Gulf War, and the suffering and death of countless Iraqi civilians in violation of the Christian definition of a "just" war.

Conveniently ignored is Israel's arsenal of nuclear weapons, its refusal to sign the Nuclear Non-Proliferation Treaty, its refusal to abide by UN resolutions, its collective punishment of Palestinians, its continued building of settlements on occupied territories, and its repeated incursions into and bombing of Lebanon.

Conveniently ignored are the U.S. use of Agent Orange in Vietnam which devastated that country which had long been a pawn of the superpowers, and the U.S. use of secret experiments on its own citizens with radiation, and chemical and biological weapons.

Conveniently ignored is the continuing need to justify the $262 billion U.S. defense budget which accounts for about 37 percent of global military expenditures. In 1996, Russia, Japan, and China each will spend about $80 billion, $42 billion, and $7 billion respectively. The six "rogue states"—Cuba, Iran, Iraq, Libya, Syria, North Korea—have a combined annual budget of $15 billion. The U.S. budget for covert operations (i.e. terrorism and support of terrorism) alone is over $29 billion.

Regardless of the facts, Col. Qaddafi remains the villain who threatens world order. We are frequently reminded that U.S. intervention is needed to extend our version of democracy, and our notions of human rights. The British empire felt it was its duty to civilize the heathen nations of the world. They devastated those nations as a result. Take the case of India and China.

Clifford D. Conner, an adjunct assistant professor of history at John Jay College of Criminal Justice, in a letter to the Editor of the *New York*

Times wrote: "In 1750, India produced almost 25 percent of the world's total manufactured goods. By 1914, India's share had dropped to 2 percent. In 1750 India's largest export was cotton textiles. By 1850, its largest export was opium, which Britain used to balance its trade with China." The British forced India to grow opium, and then they went to war with China to force it to buy the opium. The resulting famine killed about ten million Indians in this century, and many Chinese became addicted to opium.

Of course, the U.S. government cannot tell the decent folk of America its real aims outlined in 1948 by "the leading dove and peace prize winner" Mr. George Kennan for the U.S. Department of State. In his top secret *Policy Planning Study 23*, Mr. Kennan stated in part: "We have about 50% of the world's wealth, but only 6.3% of its population...Our real task in the coming period is to devise a pattern of relationships which will permit us to maintain this position of disparity...To do so, we will have to dispense with all sentimentality...We should cease to talk about vague and...unreal objectives such as human rights, the raising of living standards, and democratization."

Just over 200 years ago, on July 4, 1776, the U.S. rallied people to these marvelous words in the Declaration of Independence: "WE hold these Truths to be self-evident, that all Men are created equal, that they are endowed by their Creator with certain unalienable Rights, that among these are Life, Liberty, and the Pursuit of Happiness." The proclamation of that lofty ideal followed the holocaust of about 15 million native Americans, and has yet to be fully realized in the U.S. And beyond the shores of the U.S., presumably, these "Truths" do not apply.

[According to Robert D. Crane, principal foreign policy advisor to Richard Nixon from 1963 to 1968, President Reagan, after his attempted assassination, said that his only purpose for the rest of his life was to be an instrument of God in bringing goodness and peace to world. Adds Dr. Crane, "Completing the American revolution is another term for Islamizing the world."—"The Grand Strategy of the Great Jihad," *Middle East Affairs Journal*, Summer/Fall 1998]

May 6, 1996

Nuclear Contamination of Gulf War Battlefields Reported

The battlefields of the Gulf War are reported contaminated with nuclear materials—a by-product of the depleted uranium shells fired by U.S. tanks during Operation Desert Storm.

Depleted uranium munitions are reported to have been used in Operation Desert Storm because of their spectacular armor piercing capabilities at long distances. The 120 mm cannon shell used by the U.S. army's M1A1 Abrams tank, the 30 mm bullets used by A-10 anti-tank aircraft, the munitions used by Britain's Challenger tank, and the U.S. and British navies' Phalanx gun systems are manufactured from depleted uranium (DU).

When DU munitions explode they create microscopic airborne particles which contaminate soil, and ground and surface water for several kilometers. "They have contaminated Iraq's soil and water table with toxic and carcinogenic dust that will last 4,500 million years[?]. The dust released from these uranium tipped shells as they explode causes genetic damage and has been linked to rises in childhood cancers in Iraq" reports Hugh Livingstone of The Edge Gallery.

The Edge Gallery, London, England is planning an exhibit, documentary, and symposium on the testing, combat use, and possible health hazards of DU weapons. Gallery personnel have made several trips to Iraq where they met with the Iraqi Society for Environmental Protection and Improvement. They have also collected documents and accounts from Gulf War veterans, doctors, scientists, and environmentalists from America, Britain, Holland, and Iraq.

If the reports are correct, the use of DU in weapons is a callous solution to the nuclear industry's problem of waste disposal. In Britain and America where DU is produced as a by-product of uranium enrichment it is classified as nuclear waste subject to stringent regulations for handling and disposal. Yet as a weapon it becomes "conventional." The U.S. Department of Energy is reported to be virtually giving away the DU to munitions manufacturers.

The Gulf War was the first opportunity that U.S. and British forces had to test their DU weapons in combat conditions. There is speculation that the Gulf War Syndrome may be related to DU contamination.

June 26, 1996

Media Frenzy to Demonize Muslims

The bombing of the Khobar barracks in Saudi Arabia unleashed a media frenzy denigrating Islam, demonizing Muslims.

The same thing happened in April 1995 following the Oklahoma City bombing until two Christians were caught and charged as the alleged perpetrators. But by then the damage had been done to the Muslim community.

Over 200 incidents against Muslims were reported. However, this raised no voices against Christianity and Christians.

Now the bombing in Saudi Arabia has the *Washington Post* and others raising fears of "Islamic terrorism" and "Muslim fundamentalists." CNN blames "pro-Islam, anti-U.S." Muslims as the likely perpetrators even before law enforcement agencies have identified any suspects.

And what's Islamic about terrorism? Self defense yes, just war yes, but we find no verse in the Quran, the authoritative text on Islam, condoning terrorism. Even if the perpetrators of the Saudi bombing are Muslim, there is nothing Islamic about their act.

As for Islamic fundamentalism, the media have yet to tell us what it is. Christian fundamentalism is a term applied to doctrines which are based on a literal interpretation of the Bible. There is no parallel in Islam. Christian fundamentalism is defined in terms of the irreducible minimum of Christian belief. If pressed for an answer, we would say the irreducible minimum for being Muslim is to profess: "There is no god but God. Muhammad is the Messenger of God." In the U.S., whose constitution guarantees the free exercise of all religions, why is this a public concern?

And as for being "pro-Islam, anti-U.S.," what does that mean? Being pro-Islam has about as much to do with being pro- or anti-U.S. as it has to do with being pro- or anti-Mars!

But the U.S. media, not known for accuracy and fairness when it comes to Islam and Muslims, hide behind meaningless labels, cite the rhetoric of hatemongers, and then bemoan the divisions within the U.S. that are tearing apart the very fabric of our society. The enemy is not out there. It is here. It is among us.

July 10, 1996

Antislavery Advocates Allies in Exploitation of Sudan?

Are antislavery advocates unwitting allies in the propaganda campaign to exploit Sudan? If they're not careful, they may become just that.

Sudan is the largest country in Africa, slightly more than one-quarter the size of the U.S., and is dominated by the Nile and its tributaries. According to the CIA's *World Factbook* the ethnic background of the 30 million Sudanese is 52% black, 39% Arab, 9% others. The major religions are Sunni Muslim 70% (mostly in the north), indigenous beliefs 25%, Christian 5%. Several languages are spoken.

Sudan emerged from British colonialism and Egyptian domination on January 1, 1956 with power concentrated in the central government, and disparities among the regions. The colonial masters attempted, as in India, to exploit religious and ethnic differences to turn the North against the South; to divide and rule. In 1956, the South had one elementary school.

Since independence Sudan has had several governments. A series of conferences, sponsored by the current government, have led to plans for sharing power and resources among the 26 newly established states (previously there were 9 regions), and for addressing the issues confronting this emerging nation. Recently, Sudan has been threatened with "compulsory withdrawal" from the International Monetary Fund, and foreign intervention over allegations of slavery.

Sudan has reserves of petroleum, iron ore, copper, chromium ore, zinc, tungsten, mica, silver, and gold which the West would like to exploit. Is Sudan facing IMF sanctions because it is in arrears, or because it exceeded IMF targets for development? And, like Libya which was threatened with U.S. bombing over a weapons factory at Tarhunah (which Libya claims to be an irrigation tunnel), is Sudan being threatened with intervention over slavery to provide an excuse for Western domination or justification for U.S. defense spending which former Defense Secretary McNamara testified could safely be cut in half?

The Sudan government claims that the "slavery" is, in fact, hostage taking among rival tribes in the largely non-Muslim South which the government is trying to control. We are told this has been common practice over the ages, and the hostages (or prisoners) are usually returned or exchanged within days.

One thing is certain. No Sudanese government can justify slavery to a largely Muslim people. Islam, the faith of the Muslim people is unequivocally opposed to slavery. The first call to prayer at the Quba mosque in Madinah, built by Prophet Muhammad himself, was given by the freed slave Bilal. From its very beginning in the seventh century, much of the conversion to Islam, wrongly attributed to the sword, was because of the equality Islam offered. It is something that the U.S. only promised in 1776, began to deliver in 1964, and the promise has yet to be fulfilled.

So before the antislavery advocates rush to judgement, and support measures which may force the North-South division sought by Sudan's colonial masters, they should ask, "Are we helping the Sudanese people, or those who seek to dominate and exploit them?"

["Police have arrested a 37-year-old man in connection with claims by dozens of deaf Mexicans, rescued by authorities, who said they were forced to work for him for slave wages in New York."—Jeanne King, "NY Man Arrested in Mexican Slave-Labor Case," *Reuters*, July 20, 1997]

["Each year, 50,000 women are taken to the US to work as sex slaves, officials said. Feeder countries include Ukraine, Albania, the Philippines, Thailand, Mexico and Nigeria. Trafficking of women and children 'may be the largest manifestation of slavery in the world today,' said the panel chairman, Sam Brownback."—"Crackdown on Sex Slavery," *BBC News Online*, February 23, 2000]

July 24, 1996

TWA Flight 800: Closing the Doors on Reason

There are signs that the doors are beginning to close on logic and reason, and the propaganda machinery is cranking up to name a "culprit" in the downing of TWA Flight 800.

In it's July 23 editorial, the *Washington Post* advises that while the "evidence of terrorism is not yet there," that "courtroom-type proof" may be hard to come by, that "international validation before the act of punishment would be the best way to go, but if that is not feasible a national decision by the injured party, the United States, ought to suffice."

Within the past week, the media has also reported on Iranian efforts to purchase nuclear technologies from German firms.

The "injured party" we believe are first and foremost the passengers and crew on TWA Flight 800, second their loved ones, third TWA, and fourth, possibly, the United States. In fact, eyewitness reports suggest that the U.S. may be the guilty party. There has been nothing to link Iran, or other "rogue" states to this tragedy.

Shanti RTV of the United Kingdom reports, "One hundred witnesses have apparently already told the FBI or other law enforcement agencies that they saw an object flying through the air toward the jet, near the jet, or hitting the jet." And that "French sources reported on Sunday...that French Defense Ministry experts say it is possible that the TWA Boeing 747 which exploded last week was accidentally hit by a missile fired by a U.S. Army unit in the region." It is further reported that "the French experts believe that...the infrastructure needed to fire a missile powerful enough to hit a plane at that altitude is only possessed by army units."

There are also reports that efforts are underway to oust the Suffolk County Medical Examiner Dr. Witli, apparently a man of exceptional skill and integrity, for his reluctance to participate in a cover up. Logic and reason demand that we look at all the options as Mr. Kallstrom, the FBI agent in charge, has said.

Provided that mechanical failure is ruled out, these options may be identified, by asking, "Who gains and who loses from this tragedy?"

Those who stand to gain the most are more likely culprits than those who stand to lose the most.

A healthy dose of skepticism may also be in order. Five months after the December 21, 1988 explosion of Pan Am Flight 103 over Lockerbie, Scotland, the U.S. State Department announced that the CIA was confident that the villains were members of the Popular Front for the Liberation of Palestine led by Ahmed Jibril based in Syria. But when Syria allied with the U.S. in the Gulf War the blame was shifted to Libya.

[The *Press-Enterprise* reported today that newly disclosed evidence "points to a missile" as the cause of the explosion that killed all 230 people aboard TWA Flight 800 off New York's Long Island. The evidence includes reddish residue found on several seat backs that laboratory analysis showed to be "consistent with solid missile fuel" ingredients, the newspaper said.—*Associated Press*, March 10, 1997]

July 29, 1996

TWA Flight 800: Predictably, Media Turns on Muslims

Predictably, the U.S. media has turned on Muslims in the Middle East as likely terrorists who bombed TWA Flight 800.

CNN in its reporting today may be the first to do so, but other media pundits can't be far behind. Mr. Kallstrom, the FBI investigator in charge, says that in forty-eight hours, perhaps, the FBI may be prepared to say whether it was a bomb or missile that brought down TWA Flight 800. Does CNN know something that the FBI doesn't as to what caused the TWA plane to blow apart?

Certainly, Middle East groups should be suspect. But what about Christians in the Middle East? Christian Arabs, generally, are united with Muslim Arabs in resisting U.S. supported Israeli domination of the Middle East. And why blame "Muslims?" The bombing of the Murrah building in Oklahoma City did not elicit media voices against Christians. Muslims from the Middle East were initially blamed. The Tokyo subway gassing did not elicit media voices against Buddhists.

Blame was narrowed to a cult. Why is it that Muslims, again, are demonized?

And are Middle East groups the only ones who had the means, motive, and opportunity to bring down the TWA plane? We don't think so. If the FBI determines it was a missile that shot down the TWA plane, it is less likely, according to French authorities, that such missiles are possessed by Middle East groups.

In fact the media have been remarkably silent about coroner reports as to cause of death, and U.S. military activity in the area of the crash. In his book, *The Fire This Time*, former U.S. Attorney General Ramsey Clark says that the U.S. government bears prime responsibility for the Gulf War which was planned in Washington long before the first Iraqi soldier entered Kuwait. This was done, says Mr. Clark, to protect oil company profits, control oil supplies to Europe and Japan, and to bolster U.S. military spending.

Could it be that an accidental shoot down of the TWA plane by the U.S. military is being seized upon as another opportunity to revive the bogey of Islamic fundamentalism [Read Leon T. Hadar's, "The Green Peril: Creating The Islamic Fundamentalist Threat," and Michael Klare's *Rogue States and Nuclear Outlaws*], and to bolster defense spending? Or is it an opportunity for an attack on Libya or Iran? Just a few weeks ago the U.S. threatened to drop a nuclear bomb on an alleged Libyan weapons factory which Libya claims is an irrigation tunnel, and the Israelis have been trying to enlist U.S. support against Iran.

A responsible media should be making sure that all who had means, motive (either to commit the crime or to conceal an accident), and opportunity to down the TWA plane are thoroughly investigated. They should not be demonizing Muslims.

["In January 1997, six months after TWA Flight 800 crashed off the coast of Long Island, the Bureau of Alcohol, Tobacco and Firearms concluded that mechanical failure had caused the tragedy. But FBI officials, still convinced terrorists had downed the plane with a bomb or a missile, dismissed the 24-page report as 'unprofessional and reprehensible,' and even persuaded a Treasury Department undersecretary to help them suppress it."—Michael Grunwald, "FBI Sought to Suppress Report on TWA Crash," *Washington Post*, May 9, 1999]

August 2, 1996

Islamic Fundamentalism $500 Billion Bogey

Welfare "reform" expected to save $55 billion in six years

An extra $437 billion, the difference between what former Secretary of Defense McNamara recommended, and what will have been spent through 1996, was pumped into the Pentagon budget, from 1990 through 1996, to defend the U.S. from the bogey of Islamic fundamentalism. With interest at seven percent this amounts to over $500 billion.

To put this spending in perspective, the $266 billion U.S. defense budget for 1996 accounts for about 37 percent of global military expenditures. Russia, Japan, and China each will spend about $80 billion, $42 billion, and $7 billion. The U.S. budget for covert operations alone is over $29 billion!

Perhaps an even better perspective is gained by comparing the unnecessary $500 billion pumped into defense spending with the welfare "reform" bill which President Clinton is expected to sign. The welfare "reform" bill is expected to save $55 billion over the next six years.

September 4, 1996

U.S. Threatened to Nuke Libya Water Project

As part of the celebrations marking the 27th anniversary of Libya's September 1, 1969 revolution, Colonel Mu'ammar al-Qadhafi inaugurated the second stage of the Great Man-Made River project which last April the U.S. threatened to attack with nuclear weapons.

Labelled by the international press as the 8th Wonder of the World, the project launched in 1984 and built with the help of Korean firms includes 4000 km of pipelines, and two aqueducts of 1000 km. When completed it will bring five million cubic meters per day of water from desert aquifers to Libya's coastal cities. It will eventually increase the size of Libya's arable land by over 70 percent. The total cost of the huge project is expected to exceed $25 billion.

Because the "Jabal Nefussa" mountainous formation blocks the flow of water from the aquifers to the coast, it was necessary to drill a tunnel through the mountains and to install a pumping station at Tarhunah. This pumping station was described, according to the *Washington Post*, as a chemical plant at a Defense Department briefing on April 23, 1996 where a senior defense official stated that the United States would not exclude the use of nuclear weapons to destroy it. This plant, said the official, "is not in the interest of peace, not in the interest of stability, and not in the interest of world order." U.S. Secretary of Defense William Perry confirmed that the use of nuclear weapons to destroy this chemical weapons factory was not excluded.

Last Saturday, Presidents Alpha Omar Konare of Mali, Jerry Rawlings of Ghana, Lansana Conte of Guinea, Ibrahim Mainasara Bare of Niger and other guests including Nation of Islam leader, Louis Farrakhan, joined Libyan leader Col. Mu'ammar al-Qadhafi to simultaneously push buttons which caused a barrier to open allowing the chemical compound H_2O (aka water) to gush forth to fill the Garabouli dam, 60 km east of Tripoli, and to begin supplying water for drinking and irrigation to Libya's northwestern coastal plains.

Some intelligence services believe, however, that a chemical weapons factory does exist at Tarhunah. If so they should present their evidence to the relevant international organization for appropriate action. The Great Man-Made River project should not be threatened with nuclear strikes.

September 12, 1996

Values You May Not Want to Teach Children

U.S. foreign affairs offer a lesson in American values, but these may not be the values you want to teach your children.

Take the lessons learned from the September 3 U.S. cruise missile attack on Southern Iraq, which according to President Clinton was "to make Saddam pay a price for the latest act of brutality." The U.S. may have prevented the Iraqi brutality with a stern warning. A British newspaper, *The Independent*, said that the KDP (Kurdish party) chief Massoud Barzani warned the United States before its missile attacks that Iran was already supporting the PUK, and that his faction would turn to Baghdad for support if Washington did nothing. The paper said the KDP sent a memo to U.S. officials before the attack on Arbil saying: "Our options are limited...Since the U.S. is not responding even politically...the only option left is the Iraqis."

So when the Iraqi government goes to the aid of the KDP, which is under attack by the PUK supported by Iran, the U.S. attacks Iraq! Turkey is given the green light by the U.S. to set up a "security zone" in Northern Iraq, to attack villages and refugee camps within Iraq, and to create many thousands more refugees! And then a CIA operation to topple the Iraqi government is exposed in Iraq.

Or take the lessons learned from the Russian bombardment of the Chechens which left 40,000 dead and many more wounded. The U.S. continued to give billions in aid to Russia, interfered in the Russian elections to assure the reelection of Russian President Yeltsin, and possibly had a hand in the killing of the Chechen leader and war hero General Dudayev. It is believed that only the U.S. possesses the technology used to target and bomb General Dudayev while using a cellular phone.

Or take the lessons learned from U.S. efforts to impose sanctions on Sudan for slavery which the government of Sudan claims is hostage taking among rival tribes, and has outlawed. But the U.S. remains silent about UN reports of 25,000 to 30,000 Nepali women, many of them minor, who have been sold into prostitution in India by women traffickers. And what of the thousands who turn to prostitution, and develop AIDS, lured by the fortunes to be made at U.S. bases overseas?

Or take the lessons learned from Bosnia where a UN member country is dismembered, and massive genocide is committed. The U.S. prevents the Bosnians from defending themselves by imposing an arms embargo, replaces the Bosnian constitution with the Dayton peace accords, forces the Bosnians into an election schedule which may assure that the gains of Serbian aggression are perpetuated, and makes no serious effort to apprehend the war criminals.

Or take the lessons learned from the U.S. threats of a nuclear attack on Libya last April. The alleged Libyan chemical warfare plant in a tunnel at Tarhunah was inaugurated September 1. The "chemical weapons plant," it seems, is a man-made river bringing water from desert aquifers to Libya's coastal population.

Or take the lessons learned from the muted U.S. response to the Israeli bombing of the UN post at Qana in Lebanon, the lack of U.S. enthusiasm for enforcing UN resolutions against Israel, and U.S. efforts to deny weapons to mainly Muslim countries, while Israel stockpiles 200 to 300 nuclear warheads and 1500 kilometer range missiles, and receives over three billion dollars in U.S. aid annually.

Try explaining these lessons to your children. And the next time one of them blows away an innocent American with a handgun or Uzi, you'll know where the child learned his values.

September 13, 1996

Islamic Fundamentalism Greatest Danger to World Peace?

They won't tell you what it is or why it's so, but "Islamic fundamentalism," they say, presents the greatest danger to world peace.

Israeli leaders are quoted as saying the greatest danger the world faces is "Islamic fundamentalism." Muslim leaders fearing opposition parties echo this refrain. Newspapers in the U.S. use the phrase "Islamic fundamentalism" routinely. And the U.S. Central Intelligence Agency, perhaps indicative of it's focus on Islamic fundamentalism, placed a Muslim monument on the cover of it's *World Factbook.*

Yet we doubt if any of the reporters using this term can define "Islamic fundamentalism." Neither do they make the effort to get opposing views, nor to explain why it poses a danger to world peace, nor to ask the obvious question, "Why is it that Rev. Billy Graham, a Christian fundamentalist, is awarded the Congressional Gold Medal, appears on the cover of *Time* magazine, and dines with President Clinton, while Islamic fundamentalists are reviled in the U.S. whose constitution guarantees the free exercise of all religions?"

Christian fundamentalism, according to *Grolier's Academic American Encyclopedia,* is a term applied to doctrines which are based on a literal interpretation of the Bible. These late-19th- and early-20th-century Protestant movements opposed modern scientific theory and philosophy. With some differences, Christian fundamentalists insist on belief in the inerrancy of the Bible, the virgin birth and divinity of Jesus Christ, the vicarious and atoning character of his death, his bodily resurrection, and his second coming as the irreducible minimum of authentic Christianity.

This minimum was reflected in such declarations as the 14-point creed of the Niagara Bible Conference of 1878 and the 5-point statement of the Presbyterian General Assembly of 1910. *The Fundamentals,* a 12-volume collection of essays, was written in the period 1910-15 by 64 British and American scholars and preachers. The name fundamentalist was coined in 1920 to designate those "doing battle royal for the Fundamentals."

The infamous Scopes trial (1925) diminished fundamentalism's appeal, and by the 1950's it had moderated and become evangelicalism. In the 1970's fundamentalism was revived by televangelists (eg. the Moral Majority), and it is now represented by the "religious right" such as the Christian Coalition.

To our knowledge there is no such doctrine, or accepted definition, of "Islamic fundamentalism." The best we can determine is the definition implicit in media statements: any Muslim opposition to establishment views constitutes "Islamic fundamentalism." Perhaps that is why the purveyors of propaganda are unable to tell us what "Islamic fundamentalism" is, why it poses the greatest danger to world peace, and why they won't publish opposing views.

We are reminded of the words of Alfred McLung Lee & Elizabeth Bryant Lee in *The Fine Art of Propaganda* published in 1939, "Science flourishes on criticism. Dangerous propaganda crumbles before it."

September 27, 1996

Compassionate Banker Launches Credit for 100 Million Poor

He refuses to accept that the poor are not creditworthy. He believes that credit is a human right. This compassionate banker has launched a "microcredit" program which hopes to reach 100 million of the world's poorest by the year 2005.

While working for a bank in Bangladesh, Dr. Muhammad Yunus realized that the poorest who needed only $50 to $300 dollars to launch a small business, buy seeds, or build a home had no source of credit. By personally guaranteeing repayment, Dr. Yunus was able to persuade his bank to extend these small loans or "microcredits."

He was amazed at the results. The repayment rate for microcredits was better than for conventional loans. He was deeply moved by the changes in family lives brought about by a single sewing machine purchased to launch a new business, the tears rolling down the face of a poor woman as she entered her new $300 home, and many similar stories. But he was frustrated by his bank's reluctance to extend the program, and decided to open his own bank.

Today his Grameen Bank has a staff of 12000, and extends microcredits in 36,000 villages. How it operates breaks many banking conventions.

Instead of borrowers coming to the bank, the bank staff goes out to villages every week to extend loans and to collect payments. The Grameen Bank requires no lengthy forms, no collateral, just the signature of five women. It's focus on women is because experience has shown that women are most likely to be left out of poverty eradication programs, while they have shown themselves to be highly creative entrepreneurs and adept at saving.

The Grameen Bank's success received attention at the Earth Summit, the World Summit for Children, the Cairo Conference on Population, and the Women's Conference in Beijing. During the Beijing Conference, ABC World News Tonight named Dr. Yunus their Person of the Week.

The lessons learned by the Grameen Bank have been used in many countries, including the United States, to launch similar loan programs.

James D. Wolfensohn, President World Bank, in a letter to the Chairs of the 90 largest banks and commercial financial institutions says "Microcredit programs have brought the vibrancy of the market economy to the poorest villages and people of the world. This business approach to the alleviation of poverty has allowed millions of individuals to work their way out of poverty with dignity."

The banking revolution spawned by Dr. Yunus continues to grow. A Declaration and Plan of Action to extend the program worldwide is expected to be finalized before the February 2–4, 1997 Global Microcredit Summit in Washington, D.C. Co-Chaired by Hillary Rodham Clinton, United States First Lady; Tsutomu Hata, former Prime Minister of Japan; and Her Majesty, Queen Sophia of Spain.

December 10, 1996

If the Hutus and Tutsis Were Muslim

If the Hutus and Tutsis were Muslim, would the media identify their faith—Islam?

There is a recurring pattern of the media identifying the Muslim faith—Islam—at every negative opportunity, while not identifying the faith of non-Muslim wrongdoers. One could compile statistics for the frequency of such occurrences, but the disparities are so great that a few examples should suffice.

Oklahoma City: When terrorism "experts," based upon little or no evidence, blamed Middle Eastern terrorists for the bombing of the Murrah building, Muslims were immediately accused. Following the capture of the alleged bomber the *Washington Post* (April 22, 1995) carried a story titled "Muslim's Burden of Blame Lifts," but that burden was not placed upon Christians.

World Trade Center and Tokyo Subway: The bombing of the World Trade Center was apparently directed against U.S. support for the policies of the Egyptian government. It was identified as the act of Muslim fundamentalists. Contrast this with the poison gas attack on the Tokyo subway which was identified as the act of a "cult," but not as a Buddhist or Hindu cult which it appears to be.

Bosnia and Chechnya: The genocide of the Bosnians was described in terms of Serbs, Croats, and Muslims. Why not Orthodox Christians, Roman Catholics, and Muslims, or Serbs, Croats, and Bosnians? The brutal massacres of Chechen civilians by the Russian military was portrayed as Russia versus the Muslims of Chechnya, and not the Russian Christians against the Chechen Muslims.

TWA Flight 800: Within a week of the downing of TWA Flight 800, CNN identified Middle East terrorists as the likely perpetrators. The *Washington Post,* in its July 23 editorial, wrote that while the "evidence of terrorism is not yet there," that "courtroom-type proof" may be hard to come by, and that "international validation before the act of punishment would be the best way to go, but if that is not feasible a national decision by the injured party, the United States, ought to suffice." Regular CNN viewers and *Washington Post* readers have long been conditioned to believe that means Islamic terrorists and a Muslim country.

Afghanistan and Rwanda: The veiling of women, and keeping them from work temporarily, by orders of the Taliban in Afghanistan were identified by the media with Islam. Never mind that veils probably began with the Byzantines, and Islam is unequivocal in the equality of all mankind. Meanwhile, the brutal rapes and killings in Rwanda are merely the acts of Hutus and Tutsis.

Rwanda, according to the CIA *World Factbook*, has a population of 8.6 million which is 90 percent Hutu, 9 percent Tutsi. The religion of the people is one percent Muslim, 25 percent indigenous beliefs, 74 percent Christian.

["More than 400 people, including women and children, were feared dead last night after members of a doomsday cult set fire to themselves in a ritual mass suicide in a Ugandan church."—Wanyama Wangah, "Hundreds Feared Dead in Ugandan Mass Suicide," *Sunday Times*, March 19, 2000]

["A girl in her early teens sat in Gulu Hospital wearing a hideous grin. A victim of the Lord's Resistance Army, her lips had been snipped off in the name of God. She was a typical victim of the Christian fundamentalist cults that flourish and fight in Central Africa."—Sam Kiley, "Suicidal Credo that Came from the West," *The Times*, March 20, 2000]

June 28, 1997

Terrorism Declines: American Terrorists Deadliest

While terrorism in the U.S. is in decline, the deadliest act of terrorism in U.S. history was committed by an American veteran of the Gulf War.

According to the U.S. Federal Bureau of Investigations the most significant terrorist-related events during 1995 (the most recent year for which the annual FBI report on terrorism is available) are:

February 28, 1995—A Minneapolis jury convicted four members of a domestic extremist group, apprehended by the FBI, of violating the Biological Weapons Anti-Terrorism Act of 1989. The subjects manufactured the biological agent ricin with the intent to kill law enforcement officers.

April 19, 1995—A truck bomb destroyed the Alfred P. Murrah Federal Building in Oklahoma City, Oklahoma, killing 168 citizens and injuring hundreds. This attack was the deadliest terrorist event ever committed on U.S. soil.

October 9, 1995—A 12-car Amtrak train derailed near Hyder, Arizona. The derailment killed 1 person and seriously injured 12 others. This suspected act of terrorism is still under investigation.

November 11, 1995—The FBI prevented an act of terrorism by arresting four U.S. persons in Oklahoma for illegally conspiring to manufacture and possess a destructive device. The subjects were considering attacking civil rights offices, abortion clinics, and federal agencies.

The overall level of terrorist-related events in the United States increased, reversing last year's downturn. In 1994, there were no known terrorist acts and one small-scale suspected act in the United States.

The number of people killed in terrorist attacks in the United States increased sharply from previous years. Last year, 168 people died in a single terrorist bombing in Oklahoma City. In 1994, no American in the United States died in a terrorist attack. In 1993, six people died in the World Trade Center bombing.

July 25, 1997

Broadcasting Fairness Doctrine Promised Balanced Coverage

The passing of media ownership into fewer hands, the potential for conflicts of interests, and the virtual exclusion of significant opposing viewpoints are good reasons to reevaluate the broadcasting Fairness Doctrine, and its potential for obtaining more balanced coverage of Islam and Muslims.

The Fairness Doctrine from 1949 until 1987, when it was discontinued by the Federal Communications Commission, required broadcasters, as a condition of getting their licenses from the FCC, to cover controversial issues in their community, and to do so by offering some balancing views. It did not require equal time for opposing views. It merely prevented a station from day after day presenting a single view without airing opposing views.

The Fairness Doctrine's constitutionality was upheld by the U.S. Supreme Court in the landmark 1969 case, Red Lion Broadcasting v. FCC (395 U.S. 367). The Court ruled that it did not violate a broadcaster's First Amendment rights. Five years later, however, in Miami Herald Publishing Co. v. Tornillo (418 U.S. 241), without ruling the doctrine unconstitutional, the Court concluded that the doctrine "inescapably dampens the vigor and limits the variety of public debate." In 1984, the Court concluded that the scarcity rationale underlying the doctrine was flawed and that the doctrine was limiting the breadth of public debate (FCC v. League of Women Voters, 468 U.S. 364).

The Court's decision led to the FCC reevaluation and discontinuance of the Fairness Doctrine. The FCC stated: "We no longer believe that the Fairness Doctrine, as a matter of policy, serves the public interests. In making this determination, we do not question the interest of the listening and viewing public in obtaining access to diverse and antagonistic sources of information. Rather, we conclude that the Fairness Doctrine is no longer a necessary or appropriate means by which to effectuate this interest. We believe that the interest of the public in viewpoint diversity is fully served by the multiplicity of voices in the marketplace today and that the intrusion by government into the content of programming occasioned by the enforcement of the doctrine unnecessarily restricts the journalistic freedom of broadcasters. Furthermore, we find that the Fairness Doctrine, in operation actually inhibits the presentation of controversial issues of public importance to the detriment of the public and in degradation of the editorial prerogative of broadcast journalists."

In 1987, a bill to place the Fairness Doctrine into federal law passed the House by 3 to 1, and the Senate by nearly 2 to 1, but it was vetoed by President Ronald Reagan. Among those voting for the bill were Rep. Newt Gingrich (R-Ga.) and Sen. Jesse Helms (R-N.C.). In 1989, the Fairness Doctrine easily passed the House again, but didn't proceed further as President George Bush threatened to veto it. In 1991, hearings were again held on the doctrine, but President Bush's ongoing veto threat stymied passage.

Then the Corporation for Public Broadcasting was assigned the responsibility to: "facilitate the full development of public telecommunications in which programs of high quality, diversity, creativity, excellence, and innovation, which are obtained from diverse sources, will be made available to public telecommunications entities, with strict adherence to objectivity and balance in all programs or series of programs of a controversial nature." The "Fairness in Broadcasting Act of 1993" was sponsored in the Senate (S. 333) by Ernest Hollings (D-S.C.), and in the House (H.R. 1985) by Bill Hefner (D-N.C.).

Opponents of the Fairness Doctrine have included New York Governor Mario Cuomo, and broadcaster Rush Limbaugh. Cuomo argued that, "Precisely because radio and TV have become our principal sources of news and information, we should accord broadcasters the utmost freedom in order to insure a truly free press." Limbaugh argued that there should be no government fairness standards on broadcasters, since there are none on the print press.

Others, such as columnist Jeff Cohen, say these arguments miss the key difference: If you set up your competing broadcast station next to a Limbaugh station on the radio dial, without acquiring a government license, you will be prosecuted. Broadcast frequencies are limited, and they belong to all Americans.

Since these attempts to reinstate the Fairness Doctrine, media ownership has passed into fewer and fewer hands. Mark Crispin Miller, professor of Film and Media Studies at Johns Hopkins University, has written extensively on the media and the increasing concentration of ownership of media companies in the United States. Miller has created charts that trace the holdings of four major conglomerates: Time Warner, Disney/Cap Cities, General Electric, and Westinghouse. Each of these conglomerates owns a news network, CNN, ABC, NBC, and CBS, respectively. And not only do they own news networks, but also radio stations, magazines, cable TV, motion pictures, music, and newspapers. Furthermore, the (non-media) holdings of these conglomerates create "alarming conflicts of interests" says Miller.

Lastly, diverse opposing voices are virtually excluded from major TV networks. Among these are prominent speakers such as former U.S. Attorney General Ramsey Clark, the prolific writer Noam Chomsky, the militant National Alliance, and Muslims who by the year 2000 will constitute America's second largest religion—Islam.

More recently the Broadcasting Act of 1996 establishes the Broadcasting Standards Commission. In effect, this merges the Broadcasting Standards Council and the Broadcasting Complaints Commission, creating a single forum for public concerns relating to the portrayal of sex and violence and matters of taste and decency in television and radio programs, as well as unjust and unfair treatment and unwarranted infringement of privacy by broadcasters.

The reasons that led to the demise of the Fairness Doctrine no longer exist. Perhaps it's time to resurrect the Fairness Doctrine.

[The Muslim community, virtually unrepresented in U.S. media, now has the opportunity to enter the field of broadcasting. The FCC replaced a 30-year-old equal employment opportunity program that was struck down as unconstitutional in 1998 by the U.S. Court of Appeals for the District of Columbia. "Under the new system, the FCC will require broadcasters to have an active outreach program for hiring women and racial minorities. The companies will have to publicize job openings widely to ensure that minorities and women hear about and can compete for the positions."— John Schwartz, "FCC Unveils New Rules on Hiring," *Washington Post*, January 21, 2000]

October 6, 1997

Little Western Outrage over Israeli Terrorism

There is little or no outrage in Western capitals, academia, or media about the latest act of terrorism in the Middle East.

The incontrovertible facts regarding Israel's September 25 attempt to assassinate Hamas leader Khaled Meshal are: Israeli Prime Minister Benjamin Netanyahu himself directed the effort; a chemical or biological agent was used in the attempt to poison Meshal; the Israeli agents were using forged Canadian passports in Amman, Jordan where the assassination attempt took place; and the Israeli agents were caught by Meshal's bodyguards in the scuffle and chase that followed the assassination attempt.

There is nothing new about Israeli acts of terrorism. On the same day that the attempted assassination took place the *Associated Press* reported that a "retired army major, trying to explain why he killed a British tourist, told a court he was traumatized by service in a secret [Israeli] army unit that hunted and executed suspected Palestinian militants."

And there is nothing new about the absence of outrage in Western capitals, academia, or media regarding Israel's acts of aggression and terrorism, while their leaders wax eloquently about the West's war on terrorism.

Canada is to be commended for recalling its ambassador to Israel for consultation.

Also to be commended are fair-minded Jews and Christians who have spoken out against Israeli and U.S. policies in the Middle East such as Rabi Lerner—editor of *Tikkun*, the editors and authors of *Washington Report on Middle East Affairs,* and Rabi Schwartz whose organization, in a September 30 advertisement in the *New York Times*, condemned Zionism as a "conspiracy against Jewish tradition, and...the archenemy of the Jewish people."

["Although its aircraft bombed three Lebanese power stations...Western press and television reports almost unanimously portrayed the latest violence in Lebanon as a war by Israel in defence of its civilians on the other side of the frontier."—Robert Fisk, "How America Swallows the Israelis' Lies," *The Independent*, February 14, 2000]

November 3, 1997

U.S. Using UN Asks Iraq for the Impossible

Once again the United States and Iraq are headed toward a military confrontation that is neither reasonable nor necessary. Furthermore, U.S. insistence on asking United Nations inspectors and/or Iraq to do the impossible reveals U.S. bias, and continues to discredit and undermine the UN.

A diplomat in Baghdad reports that "Iraq today turned away in a polite way three Americans who were with a United Nations arms-inspection team arriving from Bahrain." However, Iraq emphasizes that its quarrel is with the U.S., not the UN.

The U.S. and the U.K., on the contrary, have repeatedly said that the Iraqi challenge is to the UN as a whole. They do not rule out military action. "U.S. forces are always ready," said General Anthony Zinni, who commands U.S. forces in most of the Middle East. He added, "The situation in the Gulf is tense even now. The possibility that operations could be conducted in our region is very real."

UN inspectors and/or Iraq are being asked to prove that all weapons of mass destruction have been eliminated. As any competent science student knows, the nonexistence of something, in this case Iraq's weapons of mass destruction, cannot be proven. In any case, the dispute is between Iraq and the UN. Unilateral U.S. military action being urged by U.S. Congressmen is indicative of the extent to which the UN has become a mere pawn of the U.S.

According to former U.S. Attorney General Ramsey Clark, about 10,000 Iraqis die each month as a direct result of UN sanctions. In a letter last year to the UN Mr. Clark stated, "The history of this violent century does not reveal a more deadly, cruel, inhumane and degrading torture of the whole population of an entire nation inflicted by foreign power for so long a period of time. That the deed is done in the name of the United Nations Security Council demonstrates its cowardly surrender to the will of the United States and defeats hope that the United Nations will fulfill its promise of faith in fundamental human rights, in the dignity and worth of the human person and save succeeding generations from the scourge of war."

U.S. courts of law permit the accused to have some say in the selection of judge and jury. Iraq should be accorded the same right.

November 7, 1997

Sudan: Villain or Victim of Religious Persecution?

This November 4 President Clinton signed an Executive Order imposing comprehensive economic sanctions on Sudan. The White House took this step despite little or no evidence to support its allegations against Sudan, and ample evidence that such sanctions hurt American business and the indigenous poor.

The U.S. action is a direct consequence, alleges The White House, of the "Sudanese regime's sponsorship of international terrorism, its efforts to destabilize neighboring countries, and its abysmal human rights record, including the denial of religious freedom. As a result of these sanctions, Sudanese assets in the U.S. are now blocked. The sanctions also prohibit a wide range of financial transactions between the U.S. and Sudan."

Sudan, the largest country in Africa, is charged with sponsorship of international terrorism. What acts of terrorism? The White House does not say. Is Sudan training terrorists or is it merely guilty of having provided military training to persons who then happened to commit an act of terrorism? Reliable facts and statistics are hard to come by.

Sudan is charged with efforts to destabilize neighboring countries. But on November 10, 1996 the *Washington Post* revealed that the U.S. government had provided $20 million to anti-Sudanese forces. And last January the Sudan government charged that it was being invaded on three fronts by troops from neighboring Ethiopia, Eritrea, and Uganda. Antigovernment Sudanese rebels have long been operating from bases in these three states, and striking across the border. This time, however, the invaders were well-armed and backed by tanks and artillery.

Sudan is charged with having an abysmal human rights record, including the denial of religious freedom. Sudan, a mostly Muslim country, has a Christian of the Dinka tribe, George Kungor, as its Vice President. It collects the Islam mandated zakat, or wealth tax, from Muslims only, but uses the tax to serve all its needy people—Muslim and Christian. And, we suspect, more churches are burned right here in the U.S. than in Sudan.

"South Sudan is," reports Eric Margolis in the January 27, 1997, issue of *The Toronto Sun*, "inhabited by animist or Christian Nilotic tribesmen who still live in the Iron Age. The two disparate parts of Sudan have been in conflict for decades. In the 1960s and 70s, Israel and Ethiopia armed south Sudanese rebels in an effort to destabilize the government in Khartoum. Oxfam and other Christian 'missionary' and 'humanitarian' groups raised money and provided arms to the Sudanese rebels—which they do to this day in an effort to prevent the spread of Islam."

However, the rebels in the mostly Christian south do not seem to discriminate between their perceived enemies—Christian or Muslim. On August 27, 1996, *Reuters* reported, "Three Australian Catholic nuns..., aged between 52 and 73, are being held with three other missionaries by the Sudan People's Liberation Army (SPLA)...accused by the rebels of spying and being agents of Islam because of a quotation from the Koran found by the rebels on a bookmark in a Bible belonging to the nuns." Apparently the situation there has improved. On April 21, 1997 the government concluded a peace agreement with the Christians of Southern Sudan.

The Egyptian's and British have been trying to control Sudan since the opening of the Suez Canal on November 17, 1869. They suffered a humiliating defeat on January 26, 1885 when Sudanese forces led by the Islamic mystic Ahmad ibn Abd Allah, better known as the Mahdi, recaptured Khartoum from the British led Egyptian troops, and killed General Charles Gordon in that battle. It appears that some in England have neither forgiven nor forgotten.

The London-based Sudan Foundation has been trying to engage Baroness Cox, Deputy Speaker of the House of Lords and a leading opponent of Sudan, in an open debate on allegations of slavery in Sudan. "On considering often exactly the same evidence, the Sudan Foundation and Christian Solidarity International have reached exactly opposite conclusions. One must be mistaken," says Sean Gabb, Director, The Sudan Foundation.

This coming November 16, 1997, Christian Solidarity International, evangelical churches, and sympathetic Zionists, sensing an opportunity for their anti-Islam campaign, will give voice to the "growing persecution of Christians." The goal of their "1997 International Day of Prayer for the Persecuted Church is to shatter the silence and end apathy—in the church and in the world."

We welcome an end to apathy. Terrorism, according to Websters, is "the act of terrorizing; use of force or threats to demoralize, intimidate, and subjugate, especially such use as a political weapon or policy." Let us examine the facts, engage in debate, get our priorities right. Perhaps, then the Muslim victims of Bosnia, Chechnya, Kashmir, the Philippines, and all victims of religious persecution anywhere may have hopes for peace. As Alfred McLung Lee and Elizabeth Bryant Lee said in *The Fine Art of Propaganda*, "Science flourishes on criticism. Dangerous propaganda crumbles before it."

Is Sudan the villain or the victim? Only a full and open debate will tell us the truth. Sanctions will hurt Sudan's poorest, and American business.

["In conclusion, I found that after several years of interest in this issue, which has included visits to Kordofan, the allegations of slavery made against the government of Sudan are unfounded. It is additionally clear that there has been something of an international campaign to isolate Sudan by means of these allegations. I echo the concerns of several international human rights organizations which have condemned the inflammatory nature of these allegations and I question the motivation behind them.

It is my sincere hope that the British government will look at the reality of the situation in Sudan as distinct from the view put forward by Christian Solidarity International and I hope also that CSI will distance itself from those with a political axe to grind who have compromised its good intentions."—Lord McNair, *The McNair Report on Slavery and Slavery-like Practices in Sudan*, November 1997. Lord McNair is a Liberal Democrat member of the House of Lords, England]

["An oil field near the civil war front line last month began pumping crude for export, with the help of a private Canadian company, Talisman Energy Inc., and the governments of China and Malaysia."—Karl Vick, "U.S., Rebels, Urge More Peace Talks For Sudan," *Washington Post*, October 24, 1999]

January 26, 1998

Iraq Crisis a Sham, Israel Poses Bigger Threat

The so-called "crisis" in Iraq is a sham created by Israel to divert attention from its long standing violations of UN resolutions, its blocking of the peace process, and its own weapons of mass destruction, and by the U.S. military, industrial, intelligence, congressional (MIIC) complex to justify the defense budget which could safely have been cut in half following the collapse of the Soviet Union.

The "crisis" arose when Iraq refused UN inspectors access to palaces and other sites, and asked the UN for a freeze on inspections until the matter had been discussed further at the UN. True, Iraq has stalled UN inspectors, but the stalling is not totally without justification. U.S.-led UN inspectors have turned what should have been an unbiased fact finding mission into a personal vendetta to unseat President Saddam Hussein. Mr. Hussein is no role model, but whether he remains in office or not is for the people of Iraq to decide. And, certainly, no country that professes democracy should be advocating his assassination.

As a direct consequence of this vendetta thousands have died, and are dying, in Iraq. Former U.S. Attorney General Ramsey Clark, in a May 1, 1996 letter to United Nations Ambassadors, wrote, "The entire population of Iraq has suffered. Millions will not overcome the effects of the sanctions in their lifetimes which have been shortened by years. The history of this violent century does not reveal a more deadly, cruel, inhumane and degrading torture of the whole population of an entire nation inflicted by foreign power for so long a period of time." Bishop Gumbleton of Detroit who, with more than 50 others, began a fast on January 20, 1998, implored the president and the leaders of the UN to end the sanctions. "I have never seen such devastation," he said.

UN inspectors have already concluded that Iran possesses no nuclear weapons, and its ability to produce them has been drastically set back. U.S. insistence that Iraq prove that no more weapons of mass destruction exist is an impossible task—any competent student of science knows that the nonexistence of something cannot be proved.

As for chemical and biological weapons, Alan P. Zelicoff, technical adviser to the U.S. delegation to the Biological and Toxin Weapons

Convention (BTWC), states in the *Washington Post*, January 8, 1998, that inspections are "costly and probably self-deceptive" because "in just a few days or weeks, biological weapons can be manufactured in militarily significant quantities in a site no larger than a house." Furthermore, the U.S. itself has "advocated two useful measures for the BTWC: investigations if there are unusual outbreaks of disease (such as occurred in the Sverdlovsk anthrax outbreak of 1979) and similar on-site inspections if a party to the convention alleges that biological weapons have been used." If this is what the U.S. has advocated at the BTWC, why not apply this to Iraq instead of declaring a crisis, and preparing for war.

Also, Iraq is not the only country that possesses and/or has used chemical and biological weapons. The U.S. used Agent Orange to deadly effect in Viet Nam, CS gas in Waco, and supported Iraq in its eight year war with Iran—after Iraq had used poison gas on the Kurds. Israel has chemical and biological weapons, and used them just a few weeks ago in an assassination attempt in Jordan. To say that Iraq is more likely than others to use such weapons is either self-serving propaganda, racism, or bigotry.

Israel's weapons of mass destruction are seldom cause for concern, either by the MIIC complex or the U.S. media. Israel, the largest recipient of U.S. aid, has not signed the nuclear Non-Proliferation Treaty (NPT), and has built up a formidable arsenal that raises legitimate security concerns for other nations in the region. Israel has also shown that it will use its military might to strike first, as it did in 1981 on Iraq's Osirak nuclear power plant, a legitimate facility under the NPT. It was this action against an NPT signatory, supported by the U.S., that radicalized Iraq.

Eric Margolis writing for the *Toronto Sun* reports, "Ever since the 1991 Gulf War, Syria, Iran, Egypt and Iraq have been struggling to build offensive missile capability in the face of Israel's growing nuclear arsenal. Israel is estimated to have as many as 400 atomic and hydrogen weapons. The Israeli Air Force has three squadrons equipped with Jericho nuclear-tipped missiles at the Sedot Mikha base, 45 km south of Tel-Aviv. The Jericho's can reach all major Arab cities, Iran, and Russia. Israel also has a large number of gravity nuclear weapons, possibly including neutron bombs. Further enhancing Israel's power, the U.S. is supplying it with the long-ranged F-15F. This deadly strike aircraft, air refueled, can deliver nuclear weapons from Morocco to Pakistan."

If failure to abide by UN resolutions is the criteria, action against Israel is long overdue. UN Resolution 242 passed on November 22, 1967 underscores the "inadmissibility of the acquisition of territory by war." All U.S. administrations from President Johnson's time supported this position. President Bush was the first to back away from this position, and under President Clinton the U.S. foreign policy establishment capitulated to Israeli interests. One has only to look at the backgrounds of President Clintons closest advisors, the State Department, the National Security Council, and House and Senate Foreign Relations committees to see why Israeli transgressions receive little meaningful censure, and those of the Arabs are magnified.

Israel has found an ally in the MIIC complex, which seeking to justify its bloated and unnecessary spending for "defense," is on the offensive seeking enemies.

Following the collapse of the Soviet Union, former Defense Secretary McNamara, in his 1989 testimony before the Senate Budget Committee, stated that defense spending could safely be cut in half over five years. For the Pentagon it was a simple choice: either find new enemies, or cut defense spending.

Topping the list of potential new global bogeymen were the Yellow Peril, the alleged threat to American economic security emanating from East Asia, and the so-called Green Peril (green representing Islam). The Pentagon selected "Islamic fundamentalism" and "rogue states" as the new bogeymen (see *The Green Peril: Creating The Islamic Fundamentalist Threat* by Leon T. Hadar, and *Rogue States and Nuclear Outlaws* by Michael Klare in The Wisdom Fund, Private Library at www.twf.org).

Unlike Christian fundamentalism, defined in *The Fundamentals*, a 12-volume collection of essays written in the period 1910–1915 by British and American scholars, there is no doctrine of Islamic fundamentalism, and the six "rogue states"—Cuba, Iran, Iraq, Libya, Syria, and North Korea—have a combined annual military budget of $15 billion (current U.S. budget about $265 billion). Nevertheless, an extra $437 billion, the difference between what Mr. McNamara recommended and what will have been spent through 1996, was pumped into the Pentagon budget to defend the U.S. from these bogeymen. With interest at seven percent this amounts to over $500 billion in unnecessary "defense" spending between 1990 and 1996.

To conclude, there is no crisis in Iraq which requires military action. Legitimate security concerns may be resolved by UN inspectors using criteria that the U.S. advocated at the BTWC. It is long past time to end the sanctions on Iraq.

February 20, 1998

Israel's Weapons of Mass Destruction

"No other country is in the same league in military spending as the United States," reports the Center for Defense Information (CDI). And based upon statistics provided by the CDI, no country in the Middle East has more weapons of mass destruction than Israel. And no other country in the world has escaped scrutiny of its nuclear arsenal as has Israel.

The U.S. $265 billion military budget request for 1998 is five and one-half times that of the second largest spender, Russia. According to CDI, "It is nearly eighteen times as large as the combined spending of the seven countries often identified by the Pentagon as our most likely adversaries (North Korea, Iran, Iraq, Libya, Syria, Sudan and Cuba), and the United States and its close allies spend far more than the rest of the world combined. They spend more than thirty-three times as much as the seven potential 'enemies' combined!"

"For 45 years of the Cold War we were in an arms race with the Soviet Union. Now it appears we're in an arms race with ourselves," says Admiral Eugene Carroll, Jr., U.S. Navy (Ret.), Deputy Director CDI.

As for countries possessing nuclear weapons, CDI estimates the following strategic and nonstrategic weapons: China (434), France (482), India (60+?), Israel (100+?), Pakistan (15-25?), Russia (13,200-20,200), United Kingdom (200), United States (15,500). CDI takes these total figures from Leonard Spector's, *Tracking Nuclear Proliferation*. Estimates of Israel's nuclear weapons by others are as high as 400 warheads. Reports have also surfaced that Israel is working jointly with the U.S. on a neutron bomb. Israel has not signed the nuclear Non-Proliferation Treaty. Iraq has, and there is no evidence that it has nuclear weapons.

CDI says, "The highly capable and well-equipped Israeli air force would more than suffice in the nuclear weapons delivery role, particularly with U.S.-supplied aircraft such as the F-4E and F-16. However, Israel has also produced ballistic missiles, against which its potential enemies have no defense. The Jericho I suffices for its immediate adversary of Syria, and the Jericho II brings the entire Middle East under Israel's range, particularly Iran. The Shavit space-launch booster could also be adapted to a long-range nuclear delivery role, and given the decision, Israel would be able to develop an intercontinental ballistic missile."

The UN inspectors in Iraq have found no evidence that Iraq has missiles with a capability greater than the 90 miles permitted by the Gulf War cease-fire agreement. At the CNN televised meeting in Columbus, Ohio on February 18, Secretary of State Madeleine Allbright stated, "UNSCOM has uncovered and destroyed more of those deadly weapons than were demolished during the entire Gulf War."

Secretary Allbright also said in Columbus, Iraq "has fired these missiles against four of his neighbors—Saudi Arabia, Bahrain, Iran and Israel." She was talking of the scuds for which there is no evidence that any are left in Iraq's arsenal.

Defense Secretary William Cohen, holding up a picture taken of an Iraqi mother and child killed by Iraqi nerve gas stated, "This is what I would call Madonna and child Saddam Hussein-style." Has he forgotten the pictures of the charred remains of the women and children gassed and burned in Waco, Texas, by the U.S. government?

Has Secretary Cohen forgotten that the U.S. backed Iraq in its use of gas in the war with Iran? Robert Fisk, the British journalist who has covered the Middle East for years, wrote in the London based *Independent* on February 13, "The French had sold Saddam Mirage jets. The Germans had provided him with the gas that had me almost wretching on the train from Ahwaz. The Americans had sold him helicopters for spraying crops with pesticide (the "crops," of course, being human beings). The British gave Saddam Bailey bridges. And I later met the Cologne arms dealer who flew from the Pentagon to Baghdad with U.S. satellite photos of the Iranian front lines—to help Saddam kill more Iranians."

As for Iraq's remaining chemical and biological weapons, Alan P. Zelicoff, technical adviser to the U.S. delegation to the Biological and Toxin Weapons Convention, states in the *Washington Post*, January 8, 1998, that inspections are "costly and probably self-deceptive" because "in just a few days or weeks, biological weapons can be manufactured in militarily significant quantities in a site no larger than a house." Furthermore, the U.S. itself has "advocated two useful measures for the BTWC: investigations if there are unusual outbreaks of disease (such as occurred in the Sverdlovsk anthrax outbreak of 1979) and similar on-site inspections if a party to the convention alleges that biological weapons have been used." If this is what the U.S. has advocated at the BTWC, why not apply this to Iraq?

Secretaries Allbright, Cohen, National Security Advisor Berger, and the media portray Israel as the helpless victim, and Iraq as a world threat. It is Israel's weapons of mass destruction that threaten the countries of the Middle East, and fuel the arms race. Israel's "1981 bombing of Iraq's Osirak nuclear research facility near Baghdad,...with U.S.-made warplanes and direct U.S. assistance helped radicalize Iraq," writes former U.S. Congressman Paul Findley in *Deliberate Deceptions*.

At the February 18 meeting in Columbus, CNN moderator Judy Woodruff said, "Former President Carter, was quoted yesterday as saying that up to a hundred thousand innocent Iraqi civilians could be killed." Will bombing Iraq help bring peace to the Middle East? We think not. A principled, honest assessment of the security needs of the entire Middle East region will move us in the right direction.

March 9, 1998

Did Israel Push U.S. to Brink of Needless War?

With the most recent "crisis" with Iraq averted, and more realistic assessments of the "crisis" being reported, one has to ask, "Who pushed the U.S. to the brink of a needless war with Iraq?"

At the February 18, 1998, meeting broadcast by CNN to the world from Columbus, Ohio, Defense Secretary Cohen told us "a 5-pound bag of Anthrax" could "kill half the population of Columbus," and that President Saddam Hussein of Iraq "was working on a missile that...could travel all the way from Baghdad to as far as Paris and perhaps other capitals in Europe and one day even perhaps to the United States."

At the Columbus meeting Secretary of State Madeleine Allbright said, "The risk that the leaders of a rogue state will use nuclear, chemical or biological weapons against us or our allies is the greatest security threat we face."

And media moguls and pundits warned us of dire consequences if the world failed to stand up to "Saddam." The *New York Times* and the *Washington Post* devoted pages to the threat of Iraq's weapons of mass destruction. A dispute over inspection procedures had escalated to the virtual certainty of war.

Now the truth begins to emerge.

A British newspaper, the *Independent*, reported on March 3, 1998, "A senior American ambassador in the Middle East is reported to have told American citizens that Iraq's biological and chemical warheads were 'very ineffective' just at the moment when the U.S. and Britain were saying they posed a real threat which would justify airstrikes on Iraq."

Pictures of Israelis trying out gas masks stand out in contrast to a memo written by an American businessman who attended a briefing at the U.S. embassy in Kuwait on February 3. He reports U.S. ambassador Larocco saying: "Gas masks are not required. No one at the American embassy has gas masks and the American embassy does not recommend any. They are not even interested in finding out a source for gas masks. The main reasons for this decision are the new interceptor missiles in place in Kuwait and the fact that the biological and chemical warheads are very ineffective."

And on March 6 the *Washington Post*, in an article by Martin van Creveld reported, "Now that the Iraq crisis appears to be over, we can see it for what it truly was. In my view, the threat that Saddam Hussein presents today has been vastly exaggerated both in the United States and here in Israel. With his military force still weakened by the 1991 Persian Gulf War and his economy crippled by seven years of sanctions, the Iraqi president is incapable of mounting a serious assault on anyone by air, land or sea."

We have to ask: How could so many persons in government and media be so wrong about the threat from Iraq when The Wisdom Fund with our meager resources, and readily available facts, could see that the "crisis" was a sham as early as January 26?"

When one looks for common factors shared by key government and media players who "vastly exaggerated" the threat from Iraq, one is immediately struck by the fact that virtually all these players have close ties to Israel.

May 29, 1998

Al-Azhar, Vatican Reach Landmark Agreement

The Roman Catholic Church has reached a landmark agreement on promoting a dialogue between Christians and Muslims.

"After four years of negotiation," reports *BBC News Online*, "the first joint Islamic-Christian committee in history has been established."

The agreement was reached between Islam's most prestigious scholarly institution, Al-Azhar University and Mosque, and the Vatican's council for interreligious dialogue, headed by Cardinal Francis Arinze.

Al-Azhar is the leading center for Islam's Sunni division, which comprises 90 percent of the world's approximately one billion Muslims.

The joint committee will now work to encourage cooperation between the two religions.

Cardinal Arinze, at a dialogue hosted by the National Conference of Catholic Bishops and Catholic Relief Services, was presented "The Truth About Islam"—a 600 word introduction to Islam—by The Wisdom Fund.

June 1, 1998

Rebuffed by U.S., India and Pakistan Storm Nuclear Club

India, with its three underground nuclear tests on May 11, 1998, and Pakistan with its tests two weeks later, have stormed the exclusive nuclear club whose declared membership till now was limited to the United States, Russia, Britain, France, and China.

Both India and Pakistan now face U.S. sanctions, and the world faces the specter of nuclear proliferation. Sanctions will do damage to U.S. business interests. Yet it is U.S. business interests, and U.S. policy which are largely to blame for the emergence of India and Pakistan into the nuclear club.

India's tests, the first nuclear tests by India since 1974, came after the U.S. rejected India's terms for signing the Comprehensive Test Ban Treaty (CTBT). India asked that in return for India's signing the CTBT, the U.S. present a schedule for eliminating the U.S. nuclear stockpile. The U.S. refused India's demand.

India's demand is consistent with the 1970 Nuclear Non-Proliferation Treaty in which the five self-declared nuclear powers—the U.S., Russia, Britain, France and China—declared "their intention to achieve at the earliest possible date the cessation of the nuclear arms race and to undertake effective measures in the direction of nuclear disarmament."

Having signed the NPT the nuclear powers continued to enhance their nuclear capabilities. India and Pakistan, which did not sign the nonproliferation treaty, nevertheless, showed remarkable restraint.

The *New York Times* reported on January 17, 1988, "Up to 1977 there had been over a thousand nuclear tests by the six countries possessing bombs, the overwhelming majority of these, of course, by the United States and the Soviet Union." The *New York Times* also reported,

"The United States has concealed at least 117 nuclear explosions at its underground test site in the Nevada desert over the past quarter-century."

And now with NATO expanding, and the U.S. extending nuclear protection to Poland, Hungary, and the Czech Republic against Russia, the U.S. says that India "is not really entitled to nuclear protection from China—a China with which India shares a long, disputed border that has been the subject of a bloody war...and a China that has not only refused to enter into any nuclear arms reduction treaties but is expanding its nuclear arsenal," according to Thomas L. Friedman of the *New York Times*.

Rebuffed by the U.S. refusal to take India's concerns seriously, on May 3, 1998, India's Defense Minister George Fernandes stated, "We should not only keep the nuclear option open, but also think about exercising this option to make nuclear weapons." He spoke of strategic threats from China, from Pakistan, increasing China-Pakistan collaboration, and the transfer of nuclear and missile technology from the U.S. to China. Mr. Fernandes further stated that the "United States has officially admitted that Chinese missiles are pointed towards India."

On May 11, 1998 India "surprised" the world with five nuclear tests, and joined the U.S., Russia, Britain, France and China in the nuclear club. Israel remains the sole undeclared member.

Pakistan's response to India's nuclear test was predictable given the failure of the UN Security Council to take effective action against India, and to extend credible security guarantees to Pakistan. Pakistan has fought three wars with India since both gained independence from the British in 1947, has seen its country dismembered when East Pakistan became independent as Bangladesh, and has a continuing dispute with India over Kashmir. The UN resolution of April 21, 1948, on Kashmir calls for the withdrawal of all outside forces from the State, and a plebiscite under the control of an administrator who would be nominated by the Secretary General. India has consistently refused to hold the plebiscite. This remains the biggest hindrance to improved relations between India and Pakistan.

So India tests nuclear weapons because of its fear of China, Pakistan responds to India's tests, China fears Russian missiles, Russia fears the

U.S., and the U.S. is in an arms race with itself. "For 45 years of the Cold War we were in an arms race with the Soviet Union. Now it appears we're in an arms race with ourselves," says Admiral Eugene Carroll, Jr., U.S. Navy (Ret.), Deputy Director of the Washington based Center for Defense Information.

The U.S. $265 billion military budget request for 1998 is five and one-half times that of the second largest spender, Russia. According to CDI, "It is nearly eighteen times as large as the combined spending of the seven countries often identified by the Pentagon as our most likely adversaries (North Korea, Iran, Iraq, Libya, Syria, Sudan and Cuba), and the United States and its close allies spend far more than the rest of the world combined. They spend more than thirty-three times as much as the seven potential 'enemies' combined!"

The U.S. also remains the worlds biggest weapons proliferator. The *Associated Press*, quoting a study by the Stockholm International Peace Research Institute, reported on June 26, 1997, "Global military spending declined in 1996, but weapons exports remained stable, with the United States continuing to be the world's largest arms supplier." The U.S. supplied 44 percent of the world's arms according to the peace institute study.

And the world, no doubt, has learned a lesson from the Gulf War and subsequent events—it's still a jungle out there; only the strong survive.

The world saw the U.S. bomb Iraq back into the pre-industrial age—a punishment grossly out of proportion to the damage inflicted by Iraq on Kuwait. And, says former U.S. Attorney General Ramsey Clark regarding the sanctions imposed on Iraq by the U.S. dominated UN, "More than 1.5 million have died as a result of the sanctions, and at least 5,000 continue to die every month."

And the world saw the genocide in Bosnia and Chechnya while the U.S. dominated UN failed to act.

And the world has seen the U.S. ready to bomb Iraq again on flimsy pretexts. At the February 18, 1998 meeting broadcast by CNN to the world from Columbus, Ohio, Defense Secretary Cohen told us "a 5-pound bag of Anthrax" could "kill half the population of Columbus," and that President Saddam Hussein of Iraq "was working on a missile that...could travel all the way from Baghdad to as far as Paris and perhaps other capitals in Europe and one day even perhaps to the United States."

While Secretary Cohen was hoping to incite U.S. passions against Iraq, a British newspaper, the *Independent*, reported on March 3, 1998 that, "A senior American ambassador in the Middle East is reported to have told American citizens that Iraq's biological and chemical warheads were 'very ineffective' just at the moment when the U.S. and Britain were saying they posed a real threat which would justify airstrikes on Iraq."

And it's remarkable that with all the discussion of weapons proliferation Israel's nuclear arsenal merits little U.S. condemnation or sanctions. CDI estimates that Israel has over 100 nuclear weapons. Estimates of Israel's nuclear weapons by others are as high as 400 warheads. Reports have also surfaced that Israel is working jointly with the U.S. on a neutron bomb. And Israel has not signed the NPT.

According to former U.S. Congressman Paul Findley, Israel's "1981 bombing of Iraq's Osirak nuclear research facility near Baghdad...with U.S.-made warplanes and direct U.S. assistance, helped radicalize Iraq." Iraq, a signatory to the NPT, was in compliance with the NPT which states, "the benefits of peaceful applications of nuclear technology, including any technological by-products which may be derived by nuclear-weapon States from the development of nuclear explosive devices, should be available for peaceful purposes to all Parties to the Treaty."

Until the U.S. takes credible steps to divest its nuclear arsenal, takes a principled stand toward weapons proliferation by all nations, and forgoes its assault on other nations (see *Killing Hope* by William Blum), the nuclear club will continue to attract new members.

["Russia said today that it had ruled out any discussions on changing the 1972 Anti-Ballistic Missile Treaty at arms talks with the United States this week and linked preservation of the agreement to other treaties."—"Russia Rejects Changes in ABM Treaty," *Reuters*, March 4, 2000]

June 4, 1998

Israel Blocked CIA Reports, Helped India

Israel has been helping India with its nuclear program for about 20 years, and its agents in the CIA prevented reports of this cooperation from reaching the President.

The *Times* of London revealed today, "Cooperation in missile technology stretches back over two decades and repeated private exchanges between nuclear scientists from both countries were kept secret, according to an Indian source yesterday."

London based Shanti RTV stated that Israeli intelligence agents working for the CIA ordered CIA chiefs not to pass on the information to U.S. presidents, and to ignore covert bomb deals between India and Israel. We were told, "Israel stole the U.S. and European technology, especially military and computer technology, and exported them in an illegal and pirated form to India ready to pay the price in cash."

Yesterday, Israel's *Haaretz* reported, "Kalam [head of India's Defense Research and Development Organization] visited Israel several times...while senior Israeli scientists went on reciprocal visits to India, according to a senior Indian scientist." The paper also reported that Professor Brahma Chellaney, of Delhi's Centre for Policy Research, had visited Israel last month.

Israel's Chief of Staff cancelled a visit to India this week because, reported Yediot Aharonot. "The sense was that a visit in the wake of the nuclear tests might grant a degree of credibility to the baseless reports that Israel and India were [cooperating] on nuclear arms."

The close ties between Dr. Kalam and his Israeli counterparts suggest parallels with Israel's secret cooperation with South Africa in at least one nuclear test in the late 1970s.

["The 1979 CIA memorandum,...said, 'Israelis have not only participated in certain South African nuclear research activities over the last few years, but they have also offered and transferred various sorts of advanced non-nuclear weapons technology to South Africa.'"—David Albright and Tom Zamora, "South Africa Flirts with the NPT," *Bulletin of the Atomic Scientists*, January/February 1991]

June 25, 1998

U.S. Backed Israel Prepares to Strike Iran

Israel, using F15Is supplied by the United States, is preparing to strike Iran's nuclear and missile facilities.

The London-based Jane's Information Group predicted in its annual conflict analysis that Israel would launch a limited pre-emptive strike, and the *Times* of London reported today that Israel's potential for launching such attacks "increased substantially yesterday with the surprise announcement [by Israel's *Air Force Magazine*] that the first of its new F15I long-range strike aircraft are operational."

Israel received the first two of the $84 million F15I warplanes made by the U.S. in January, and the "$2.5 billion order for 25 of the world's most advanced fighters, plus spare parts, is due to be completed by the end of this year," reports the *Times*.

The Washington-based Center for Defense Information estimates that Israel has 100-plus nuclear weapons. Estimates of Israel's nuclear weapons by others are as high as 400 warheads. And according to CDI "Israel has also produced ballistic missiles, against which its potential enemies have no defense."

Israel's "1981 bombing of Iraq's Osirak nuclear research facility near Baghdad...with U.S.-made warplanes and direct U.S. assistance, helped radicalize Iraq," says former U.S. Congressman Paul Findley.

Iran's peaceful nuclear program is in compliance with the Nuclear Non-Proliferation Treaty which states, "The benefits of peaceful applications of nuclear technology, including any technological by-products which may be derived by nuclear-weapon States from the development of nuclear explosive devices, should be available for peaceful purposes to all Parties to the Treaty."

Israel, unlike Iran has not signed the NPT, and has been helping India with its nuclear program for about 20 years according to a June 4, 1998, article in the *Times*.

July 14, 1998

Soft Spoken Muslim Hero of World Cup

Zinedine Zidane, a soft spoken Muslim, emerged last Sunday as the hero of the World Cup soccer finals in France.

Son of an Algerian janitor, Zidane, with a flick of his head scored the first two of the three goals which gave France victory over Brazil—favored to win the 16th World Cup. With these two goals, Zidane, in the final match of the World Cup, watched by an estimated 1.7 billion television viewers around the world, became an instant celebrity.

In an impromptu celebration 1,500,000 people packed the two miles along the Champs Elysees yesterday to see their conquering heroes in the middle of a working day. A huge portrait of Zidane was projected on the Arc de Triomphe, and crowds shouted "Zidane! President!" Not since DeGaulle marched triumphantly into Paris in 1944 has France seen such a celebration.

The fact that France won the World Cup, with the "most ethnically diverse team in the competition—African, Arab, Pacific island, West Indian, Armenian, Breton, Norman, Basque, Provencal" according to the London-based *Independent*, may not change the realities of life for immigrants in late-twentieth century France.

For the moment, however, the latent racism in French society—the most racist society in Europe according to a government survey published last week, was forgotten.

"This team is France. But the improved version," said the news magazine *Marianne*. "This is the France we would love to see: valiant, stubborn, enterprising, multiracial but accepting its 'metissage' (mongrel nature) as a gentle fact of life."

["A French high school expelled nine Moslem girls on Monday for defying a government ban on wearing Islamic headscarves in class. The headmaster said 11 other girls were likely to be expelled on Tuesday for wearing the headscarves."—"French School Expels Nine Moslems in Scarf Row," *Reuters*, October 24, 1994]

["The refusal of teachers in three French schools to teach Muslim girls wearing headscarves threatens to reopen a long-running conflict between freedom of religious expression and the secular nature of the public education system."—Jon Henley, "Islamic Scarves Put Pupils On Outer," *The Guardian*, January 12, 1999]

July 25, 1998

NY Times Slants Reports, Accommodates Defense, Israel

The *New York Times* slanted its reporting of Iran's Wednesday, July 22, 1998, medium-range missile test to accommodate the defense establishment and Israeli interests.

The day following Iran's missile test, the *New York Times* front page carried a story headlined, "Iran Said to Test Missile Able to Hit Israel and Saudis." the *New York Times* reported a senior official of the U.S. government saying on Wednesday night, "The weapon, with a range of about 800 miles, is capable of hitting Israel and Saudi Arabia, and of altering the political and military balance of power in the Middle East." Surely, the *New York Times* should have asked, "Why?"

A simple "Why" would have revealed that "Israel has also produced ballistic missiles, against which its potential enemies have no defense," according to the Washington-based Center for Defense Information.

A simple "Why" would have revealed that Israel has 100 plus nuclear weapons according to CDI. Iran has none. Estimates of Israel's nuclear weapons by others are as high as 400 warheads.

A little further investigation would have revealed that, according to CDI, "The highly capable and well-equipped Israeli air force would more than suffice in the nuclear weapons delivery role, particularly with U.S.-supplied aircraft such as the F-4E and F-16. However, Israel has also produced ballistic missiles, against which its potential enemies have no defense. The Jericho I suffices for its immediate adversary of Syria, and the Jericho II brings the entire Middle East under Israel's range, particularly Iran. The Shavit space-launch booster could also be adapted to a long-range nuclear delivery role, and given the decision, Israel would be able to develop an intercontinental ballistic missile."

A little further investigation would have revealed that Israel received the first two of the $84 million F151 warplanes made by the U.S. in January, and "the $2.5 billion order for 25 of the world's most advanced fighters, plus spare parts, is due to be completed by the end of this year" as reported by the *Times* of London last month.

However, the *New York Times* neither asked "Why," nor did they report relevant facts. That, of course, would not fit the "spin" they desired to give the story.

The *New York Times*' spin on foreign affairs is usually adopted by major media. The *Associated Press* followed up on July 24 by reporting:

- Sen. Sam Brownback, R-Kan., chairman of the Senate Foreign Relations subcommittee on the Near East and South Asian Affairs, said Wednesday's test creates "a new and incredibly more dangerous environment for the Middle East."

- Sen. Richard Shelby, R-Ala., chairman of the Senate Intelligence Committee, said if Iran has a missile capable of threatening its neighbors, "what is to stop them from developing the means to deliver such a weapon upon the United States and any of our allies?"

- House Speaker Newt Gingrich, R-Ga., reiterated calls for a national missile defense system.

The same day, July 24, the *Times* of London revealed, "The Shehab 3 test [Iran's missile test] was leaked to the paper [*New York Times*] within hours of its detection by a U.S. spy satellite."

The leak to the *New York Times* by the intelligence community is part of the continuing effort by the defense establishment to justify bloated defense spending.

The U.S. $265 billion military budget request for 1998 is five and one-half times that of the second largest spender, Russia. According to CDI, "It is nearly eighteen times as large as the combined spending of the seven countries often identified by the Pentagon as our most likely adversaries (North Korea, Iran, Iraq, Libya, Syria, Sudan and Cuba). And the United States and its close allies spend far more than the rest of the world combined. They spend more than thirty-three times as much as the seven potential enemies combined!"

"For 45 years of the Cold War we were in an arms race with the Soviet Union. Now it appears we're in an arms race with ourselves," says Admiral Eugene Carroll, Jr., U.S. Navy (Ret.), Deputy Director of CDI.

To conclude, the *New York Times* used a self-serving report, leaked by the defense establishment, to slant reporting, thereby, accommodating the defense establishment and Israeli interests.

August 4, 1998

Washington Metro Displays "The Truth About Islam"

"The Truth About Islam" will be on display in Metro rail stations in Washington, DC, during the month of August.

Described by visitors to The Wisdom Fund web site as the "best, short introduction to Islam," the message is displayed in 62 by 44 inch, backlighted "dioramas" on Metro rail station platforms. The display is intended to foster harmony among people of diverse faiths. Designed for the age of the 30-second sound-bite, this unique display conveys the spirit of Islam in less than 600 words.

Since February 1995, "The Truth About Islam" has been published in *Foreign Affairs,* the *Washington Times* on the day of the Million Man March, and in other journals and community papers. It is seen by visitors from 50 to 70 countries each month at The Wisdom Fund's web site www.twf.org. Posters of "The Truth About Islam" are being displayed in homes, offices, prisons, and mosques. They have been presented to religious leaders and public officials, and are being used as teaching aids in schools and universities.

"The Truth About Islam" display may be seen during August 1998 at the following Metro rail stations: Anacostia, Fort Totten, Judiciary Square, L'Enfant Plaza, McPherson Square, Potomac Avenue, Shaw-Howard University, Stadium-Armory, U Street-Cardoza, Van Ness-UDC.

Posters of "The Truth About Islam" superimposed on a photograph of the Quba mosque, the first mosque constructed by the Prophet, are available from the web site www.twf.org—the text of the message is contained in the Appendix.

[Given widespread misunderstanding of Islam, which U.S. media has done little to dispel, this brief description of Islam—and a couple of other articles regarding Islam and/or Muslims—are included in this book for the benefit of the reader who has not been exposed to the truth about Islam.]

August 13, 1998

Kenya/Tanzania Bombs: Truth a Casualty?

Has the media moved too quickly to tie Osama bin Laden to the August 7 bombings in Kenya and Tanzania? We certainly don't know, but we hesitate to jump to hasty conclusions.

In August 1964 the rationale for the Viet Nam war seemed very clear. "American Planes Hit North Vietnam After Second Attack on Our Destroyers; Move Taken to Halt New Aggression," headlined the *Washington Post* on August 5, 1964.

That same day the front page of the *New York Times* stated: "President Johnson has ordered retaliatory action against gunboats and 'certain supporting facilities in North Vietnam' after renewed attacks against American destroyers in the Gulf of Tonkin."

But there was no "second attack" by North Vietnam—no "renewed attacks against American destroyers." "By reporting official claims as absolute truths," wrote syndicated columnist Norman Solomon on the 30th anniversary of that "attack," "American journalism opened the floodgates for the bloody Vietnam War. A pattern took hold: continuous government lies passed on by pliant mass media leading to over 50,000 American deaths and millions of Vietnamese casualties."

"Much later it was discovered," says Norman Solomon, "that rather than being on a routine patrol August 2, the U.S. destroyer Maddox was actually engaged in aggressive intelligence-gathering maneuvers— in sync with coordinated attacks on North Vietnam by the South Vietnamese navy and the Laotian air force."

In the case of the bombing of United States embassies in Kenya and Tanzania certain events merit explanation, and relevant questions need to be answered:

• How is it that the Israelis, who for some time have been seeking to attack Iran and dismember Sudan, were first on the scene? Did the Israelis contaminate the crime scene with planted evidence, or remove evidence that may point to them?

• Why was the Fairfax rescue squad, ready to travel immediately following the bombing, unable to get an airplane for 24 hours, and upon arrival in Kenya, prevented from participating in rescue efforts by the Israelis?

• Why did Israel, according to an *Associated Press* report of August 12, advise U.S. officials "to treat with skepticism a warning that the U.S. Embassy in Kenya might be the target of a bombing attack?" According to *AP*, "an Israeli security official said the Americans had asked Israeli intelligence to assess the credibility of an intelligence source who had warned of an attack."

Also, on August 12, the London-based *Independent* reported that the *East African Standard* quotes a UIIS guard, belonging to an American-based company which specializes in government security, as saying that he and other security men were engaged in a gun battle with five armed "Arab-looking" bombers who entered the rear compound. This guard, Joash Okindo allegedly claimed several colleagues were killed in a grenade attack. However, UIIS insists none of its employees died.

The *Independent* also stated, "The problem for the FBI is that if some of the "witnesses" were close enough to see what they claimed to have seen, it is a miracle they lived to tell the tale." How are these discrepancies in witness accounts explained? And could the "Arab-looking" persons be Israeli agents?

What is the evidence, and how was it obtained, that led to the speedy arrests in Tanzania of the "14 people, including six Sudanese, six Iraqis, a Somali-born Australian and a Turk," reported by the *Associated Press* on August 12?

We're told by the media that the near simultaneous bombings in Kenya and Tanzania was the work of "professionals, perhaps state sponsored." So how is it that those professionals did not plan their escape better?

What is the evidence that points to Osama bin Laden? Was bin Laden's alleged fatwah the proximate cause of the Kenya/Tanzania bombings? Paraphrasing Black's Law Dictionary: Did the fatwah in a natural and continuous sequence, unbroken by any efficient intervening cause, result in the bombings? Was the fatwah the last negligent act contributory to the bombings, without which the bombings would not have occurred?

And why is it that in the case of the bombing of the Murrah building in Oklahoma City the media gives so much detail regarding events preceding the bombing, the events following the bombing, and the backgrounds and motivation of the perpetrators, while little of this sort of detail is offered in the case of the bombings in Kenya and Tanzania?

The media, that seeks to titillate us with endless speculation in the O.J. Simpson and Monica Lewinsky matters, seems to have little appetite for critical examination of the "facts" when it comes to anything that can be pinned on Muslims.

Like the events leading to the war in Viet Nam, will truth become a casualty?

August 17, 1998

Kenya/Tanzania Bombs: Perpetrators Caught?

What are we to make of Mohammad Sadiq Howaida who has confessed to his role in the Kenya bombing, and his ties to Osama bin Laden? If past experience is a guide, either we will soon learn that Howaida's confession is bogus, or the truth may remain hidden for a long time.

About six weeks ago, following the India and Pakistan nuclear tests, Iftikhar Chaudhry, a Pakistani, managed to deceive much of the Indian and U.S. media. Chaudhry, calling himself a senior nuclear research scientist, claimed to have defected to the USA, via Canada, to protest plans by Pakistan to launch a preemptive nuclear attack on India.

The Pakistani "defector," reported Eric Margolis in the *Toronto Sun*, July 9, 1998, "was offered large sums of money by U.S. newspapers for his story. India's media trumpeted Chaudhry's allegations. So did some conservative U.S. newspapers, which have been warning of a sinister plot by Iran, China and Pakistan to target Israel with nuclear weapons." Chaudhry turned out to be a lowly bookkeeper for a bathroom tile manufacturing firm in Pakistan!

During the World Trade Center bombing trial, the *New York Times* reported that the evidence that Sheikh Rahman even knew of the plan to bomb the World Trade Center, and other buildings in New York, was scant. The government's primary witness against Sheikh Rahman was an FBI informant, Mr. Emad Salem, who confessed to lying under oath in a previous trial.

Six months before the World Trade Center bombing, the FBI terminated Mr. Salem after he failed several lie detector tests. According to the *New York Times,* following the bombing Mr. Salem was rehired for a fee of over $1 million. Sheikh Rahman, convicted in the World Trade Center bombing, may well be innocent.

[Mohammad Sadiq Howaida, also known as Abdull Bast Awadh and Mohammed Saddiq Odeh, "says Pakistani investigators refused to let him eat, drink or sleep for three days until he was pressured into a false confession."—"Bombing Suspect Alleges He Was Bullied Into Confession," *Washington Post*, September 4, 1998, p. A08]

August 19, 1998

U.S. Prepares Panama Style Assault on Bin Laden?

Is the U.S. preparing for a Panama style assault on Osama bin Laden for the August 7 bombings in Kenya and Tanzania?

Just yesterday, based on FBI statements, *Reuters* and *Associated Press* reported that Howaida, the bombing suspect picked up in Pakistan, denied his and bin Laden's involvement in the bombing. *AP* reported, "After three days of questioning, a suspect [Howaida] in the twin U.S. Embassy bombings in East Africa has not admitted any role in the crimes or implicated anyone else, the FBI said Monday."

Today, based on statements by "Pakistani intelligence officials who spent a week questioning the man," the *Washington Post* and British media are trumpeting bin Laden's involvement in the Kenya/Tanzania bombings, and terrorism around the globe. The *Washington Post*, in a front page headline reported "Suspect Details Anti-U.S. Terror Force." Does the *Post* know something the FBI doesn't?

How is it that Pakistani intelligence, seemingly so effective in apprehending suspects wanted by the U.S., can't seem to find bombers in its own back yard?

The *Reuters* story denying Howaida's involvement in the bombing seems to have disappeared from the Internet. And, apparently, U.S. and British media, and Pakistani intelligence, are ahead of the FBI in identifying the perpetrators.

What is the evidence that bin Laden, 1 of 25 children we're told, has assets valued at $300 million which are being used to finance terrorism worldwide? How is it that the U.S. has not found and frozen bin Laden's assets? Is bin Laden's wealth greatly exaggerated, as were Iraq's defenses during the Gulf War?

Is the U.S., frustrated in the investigation of the Khobar barracks bombing, about to resort to an assault on bin Laden so as to send a message to other would-be terrorists?

The timing and circumstances seem right. Pakistan could use an easing of sanctions imposed following their nuclear test. The Taliban, in Afghanistan where bin Laden is residing, seeks United Nations recognition. The reward offered following the Kenya/Tanzania bombing may loosen tongues. And President Clinton could use a break.

A Panama-style assault by the U.S., which resulted in the capture of President Noriega, and the death of about 3000 others, seems imminent. Iraq's invasion of Kuwait resulted in about 300 deaths.

["Today, I ordered our armed forces to strike at terrorist-related facilities in Afghanistan and Sudan because of the threat they present to our national security."—August 20, 1998, 2:00 PM, President Clinton]

["But now some State Department and CIA officials argue that the government cannot justify its actions."—"Decision to Strike Factory in Sudan Based on Surmise," *New York Times*, September 21, 1998]

["The White House ignored Attorney General Janet Reno when she questioned whether evidence linking Islamic extremist Osama bin Laden to the bombings of two U.S. embassies in Africa was strong enough to justify retaliatory attacks, *The New Yorker* magazine reported."—"Reno Questioned U.S. Raids," *Associated Press*, October 5, 1998.]

["Some 60,000 soldiers and police officers" have passed through the courses at "the long-notorious School of the Americas." Established in 1946, at Fort Benning, Georgia, "the drug-dealing Gen. Manuel Noriega of Panama was an alumnus, as were the Guatemalan colonel linked to the killing of an American innkeeper in 1990, 19 of the 26 soldiers who murdered a group of Jesuit priests in El Salvador in 1989, and the late Roberto D'Aubuisson, who reputedly organized many of El Salvador's death squads."—"Watching What the Army Teaches," *New York Times*, November 21, 1999]

August 24, 1998

President Clinton Fails Vision, Values Test

President Clinton has failed the fundamental test for Chief Executive Officers.

The primary function of the CEO of any organization is to define the vision and values of the organization.

After almost six years in office, President Clinton's vision for the United States remains undefined.

His values, what we know of them, are unacceptable.

August 27, 1998

U.S. Foreign Policy Invites "Terrorism"

U.S. foreign policy invites "terrorism." To end it we must end policies that create it.

Graham E. Fuller, former vice-chairman of the National Intelligence Council at the CIA, and Charley Reese, self-described "ex-soldier," now a columnist for the *Orlando Sentinel,* are right on target in their recent articles following the U.S. missile strikes on Sudan and Afghanistan in retaliation for the bombing of the U.S. embassies in Kenya and Tanzania.

Mr. Fuller writes ("Airstrikes Aren't the Endgame," *Los Angeles Times,* August 24, 1998), "It is dangerous to divorce terrorism from politics, yet the U.S. media continue to talk about an abstract war against terrorism without mention of the issues or context that lie behind them."

Mr. Reese writes ("Face It: U.S. Foreign Policy Contributes to Acts of Terrorism," *Orlando Sentinel,* August 18, 1998), "Terrorism is a political act, a response to U.S. foreign policy. It is an act of war waged by people too weak to have a conventional army or one large enough to take on the United States."

Fuller and Reese identify the realities of U.S. foreign policy, Muslim perceptions, and media obfuscation that serve to perpetuate the cycle of violence. Among these are:

• "U.S. support for almost any ruler [often against the wishes of his people] willing to protect U.S. interests—routinely identified in Washington as oil and Israel" says Fuller. And this support usually comes without meaningful input from American Muslims.

• While Muslims are virtually excluded from high-level policy making and media, "Jewish Americans," says Fuller, "occupy nearly every single senior position relating to U.S. Arab-Israeli policy."

• Reese says, "The one-sided support of Israel, even when Israel is clearly an aggressor or an abuser of human rights, creates enemies. When your wife and children are killed with U.S. weapons wielded by a government backed by the United States and protected from UN sanctions by the United States, it doesn't sit too well."

• Reese adds, "We slapped sanctions on Sudan allegedly because someone in Washington doesn't like its internal human-rights policies that, you can be sure, are far more humane than China's or those of some of the African dictators we so ardently supported. I suspect the real reason is the current government won't cut a deal on the oil discovered in Sudan many years ago."

Contrary to what U.S. media tell us, U.S. foreign policy doesn't reflect the kind, and charitable nature of the average American.

Terrorism has no place in this world. But distinguishing the freedom fighter from the terrorist is a matter of perspective. And what we call realpolitik, or power politics, is merely a euphemism for terrorism of another kind.

We have a choice: an endless war on terrorism, or following the path to a just and lasting peace. We will have embarked on the path to peace when we routinely include Muslims, of diverse views, in debates at the level that U.S. policy is made.

["The Clinton administration will not challenge a lawsuit filed by a Saudi businessman who said the bombing last year of his pharmaceutical plant in Sudan was a 'mistake' based on faulty intelligence data. The administration also agreed to release $24 million in assets that the businessman, Saleh Idris, had deposited in U.S. banks."— Jerry Seper, "U.S. OKs Payout for Sudan Bombing 'Mistake'," *Washington Times*, May 5, 1999]

September 25, 1998

Double Standard Targets Muslim Countries

Allegations of chemical and biological weapons (CBW) production by countries with a majority Muslim population receive wide dissemination, media condemnation, a cruise missile assault, and even threats of a nuclear strike. CBW production by Israel, and treaty violations by the U.S. get barely a mention.

"Hours after they launched cruise missiles at the [Sudan] factory on August 20," said the *New York Times* (September 21), "senior national security advisers described Al Shifa as a secret chemical weapons factory financed by bin Laden. But now says the *New York Times*, "State Department and CIA officials argue that the government cannot justify its actions."

Others around the world were immediately suspicious of the official rationale for the U.S. assault; it coincided with the day that Monica Lewinsky was to testify before a grand jury against President Clinton. The *New York Times* reported (August 29), "The plant made both medicine and veterinary drugs, according to U.S. and European engineers and consultants who helped build, design and supply the plant." "The Al Shifa plant," said the International Action Center (September 21), "raised Sudan's self-sufficiency in medicine from 3 percent to over 50 percent and produced enough veterinary medicine for all of Africa."

About two years ago, a pumping station at Tarhunah in Libya was described, according to the *Washington Post*, as a chemical plant at a Defense Department briefing on April 23, 1996 where a senior defense official stated that the United States would not exclude the use of nuclear weapons to destroy it. The then U.S. Secretary of Defense, William Perry, confirmed that the use of nuclear weapons to destroy this chemical weapons factory was not excluded.

The pumping station turned out to be part of what was labelled by the international press as the Eighth Wonder of the World. A project which when completed will bring five million cubic meters per day of water from desert aquifers to Libya's coastal cities. It will eventually increase the size of Libya's arable land by over 70 percent.

And need we mention the suffering of the Iraqi people. The review of sanctions imposed by the United Nations has been delayed due to traces of VX allegedly found in weapons destroyed by Iraq under UN supervision.

"Before the 1991 Gulf War, Iraq had the Middle East's most advanced and comprehensive health care system," says former U.S. Attorney General Ramsey Clark. "Now Iraq lacks even basic medicines to treat preventable diseases because of the sanctions. More than 1.5 million have died as a result of the sanctions, and at least 5,000 continue to die every month. Most of the victims are children and elderly people."

While mainly Muslim countries are targeted for condemnation and military assault, the hypocrisy of the double standard regarding weapons of mass destruction is ignored by the media.

Today, the *Times* of London reported, "Israel's High Court yesterday suspended plans by the Government of Binyamin Netanyahu to expand a top-secret scientific facility south of Tel Aviv where residents fear biological weapons are being produced, according to the local mayor."

Further, said the *Times*, "The shadowy biological institute situated in the growing suburban community of Nes Ziona...[is] believed by many foreign diplomats to be one of the most advanced germ warfare institutions in the Middle East. Israel has repeatedly accused Arab and Islamic countries hostile to it of manufacturing such weapons on a large scale, but has never admitted possessing biological or chemical weapons, just as it has never owned up to a nuclear capability, although it is an open secret that the country has at least 200 nuclear warheads."

According to the *Washington Post* (September 17), "The United States has violated the Chemical Weapons Convention since it was ratified by the Senate 18 months ago." According to the Washington based Stimson Center "To say that the United States has set a poor example under the CWC would be a vast understatement....For the past 18 months, the United States has been the malignancy in the midst of the CWC."

["Tests of Iraqi missile warheads conducted for the United Nations in Swiss and French laboratories have not found evidence of VX nerve gas."—John M. Goshko, "New Tests of Iraqi Warheads Don't Find Nerve Gas," *Washington Post*, September 28, 1998, p. A12]

October 1, 1998

Should U.S. Bomb Israel's Chemical, Biological Plant?

Should the U.S. bomb Israel's top-secret chemical, biological plant south of Tel Aviv?

The *Times* of London has reported (September 25) the existence of a "shadowy biological institute situated in the growing suburban community of Nes Ziona...believed by many foreign diplomats to be one of the most advanced germ warfare institutions in the Middle East."

Today, *Associated Press* reported that an "Israeli cargo jet that crashed in Amsterdam six years ago was carrying chemicals used to produce the deadly sarin nerve gas." According to reports Wednesday in a Dutch newspaper, the respected national daily *NRC Handelsblad*, the El Al plane was carrying 50 gallons of the chemical dimethyl methylphosphonate from "an American company in Pennsylvania and was headed for the Israel Institute for Biological Research in Ness Ziona near Tel Aviv." Hundreds of residents in the neighborhood surrounding the crash site are suffering health problems say Dutch newspapers.

Last year, on September 25, Israeli agents in Jordan attempted to assassinate Hamas leader Khaled Meshal. Israeli Prime Minister Benjamin Netanyahu himself directed the effort, and a chemical or biological agent was used in the attempt to poison Meshal.

"Israel has repeatedly accused Arab and Islamic countries hostile to it of manufacturing such weapons on a large scale," said the *Times* (September 25), "but has never admitted possessing biological or chemical weapons, just as it has never owned up to a nuclear capability, although it is an open secret that the country has at least 200 nuclear warheads."

At the urging of Israel's friends in Washington, on August 20 this year, the U.S. launched cruise missiles at the Al Shifa pharmaceuticals factory in Sudan. Described by senior national security advisers as a secret chemical weapons factory, plant designer Henry R. Jobe from the U.S., British technical manager Tom Carnaffin, who supervised construction from 1992-96, and Jordanian engineer Mohammed Abul Waheed, who supervised plant production in 1997, have all testified that it would have been impossible for this plant to have produced chemical weapons. "State Department and CIA officials argue," reported the

New York Times (September 21), "that the government cannot justify its actions."

Should the U.S. bomb Israel's top-secret chemical, biological plant? If you want to get reelected in the U.S., don't even think about it. Israel isn't the Sudan.

["Israeli assault aircraft have been equipped to carry chemical and biological weapons manufactured…at the Institute for Biological Research in a suburb of Nes Ziona 12 miles southeast of Tel Aviv."—Uzi Mahnaimi, "Israeli jets equipped for chemical warfare," *Sunday Times*, October 4, 1998]

October 6, 1998

Washington Post Slams "Asian Values"

The *Washington Post*, Sunday, October 4 editorial, "Malaysian Justice," slams the values of Asia—a large, diverse continent, and birthplace of all the major world religions.

The *Post* states in the opening sentences, "The true face of 'Asian values' appeared in a Malaysian courtroom a few days ago. It was the face of Anwar Ibrahim, his eye blackened from a police beating…" Prime Minister Mahathir Mohammad is alleged to be responsible for the beating.

Asia, largest of the earth's seven continents, covers about one-third of the world's total land area. It has more than 3.2 billion inhabitants, and accounts for three-fifths of the world's population.

According to Microsoft's *Encarta*, Asia is bounded by the Arctic, Pacific, and Indian oceans. The Ural Mountains in Russia form the boundary between Asia and Europe. Asia and Africa are separated by the Red Sea. The *Encarta* also states as follows:

"Asia is divided for convenience into five major realms: the areas of the former Union of Soviet Socialist Republics; East Asia, including China, Mongolia, Korea, and Japan; Southeast Asia; South Asia, including the Indian subcontinent; and Southwest Asia, including much of the Middle East."

"The continent may also be divided into two cultural realms: that which is Asian in culture (East Asia, Southeast Asia, and South Asia) and that which is not (Asia of the former U.S.S.R., and Southwest Asia)."

Asia is the birthplace of all the major world religions: Buddhism, Christianity, Confucianism, Hinduism, Islam, Judaism, and Taoism.

If as the *Post* says the face of Anwar Ibrahim, his eye blackened from a police beating, represents the true face of "Asian values," then does not the Clinton-Lewinsky affair represent the true face of "American values?"

Of course not. The behavior of one person, regardless of how prominent that person or despicable the act, does not define the values of the larger population.

November 3, 1998

Arafat Salutes Sharon, Surrenders Palestinians

Palestine Liberation Organization Chairman Yasser Arafat rose to salute Israeli foreign minister Ariel Sharon as he entered the conference room at the Wye River Plantation to begin discussions intended to revive the stalled land for peace process begun in Oslo. In the following days, the salute would symbolize Arafat's surrender of the Palestinians to the Israeli occupation forces, and of his legitamacy as a leader.

Under the Wye River agreement announced on October 23, for which Israel and the PLO are to receive substantial U.S. aid, Arafat agreed to step up "antiterrorist efforts" in the West Bank, and to eliminate anti-Israel provisions in the PLO founding charter. The Israelis would cede 13 percent more of the territory on the West Bank, and release 750 of the 3000 political prisoners held without trial in Israeli jails.

Arafat's "antiterrorist efforts," to be monitored by the U.S. Central Intelligence Agency, are intended to further crackdown on Palestinians opposed to the agreement. Arafat agreed to disarm about 10,000 of the PLO police force, stifle dissident voices, and step up arrests following any attack on Israelis, or on the basis of "evidence" provided by Israel.

Whether guilty or innocent, those arrested are not likely to receive either justice or humane treatment. Amnesty International has faulted the Palestinian Authority and Israel on human rights. *Associated Press*, September 10, 1998, reports, "Israel and the Palestinian Authority have consistently violated human rights in the name of security in the five years since they signed their first peace agreement." There are no provisions in the Wye River agreement for the arrest of militant Israelis.

Israel will continue its policy of settlement expansion, and the demolition of Palestinian homes—a policy which has provoked retaliation by the Hamas resistance, and a further crackdown by Arafat on his own people. In the days following the Wye River agreement, Arafat's forces muzzled Sheikh Yassin, Hamas' spiritual leader, and arrested about 300 Hamas resistors.

The Wye River agreement gives the Palestinians little that was not already promised by Israel under the Oslo accords. Netanhayu appears to have shifted from his opposition to the Oslo accords, but may be using the agreement to raise the standards to be met by the Palestinians, and has delayed Israeli troop withdrawal.

Arafat's surrender may provoke reprisals against the Palestinian Authority. *Associated Press*, November 1, 1998, reported, "The [Palestinian] Authority's security apparatus, its officials and elements, will never be safe" from Hamas' vengeance, said a Washington leaflet faxed to news organizations that was signed by the Izzedine al Qassem brigades, Hamas' military arm.

"Israel's internal security service has warned Benjamin Netanyahu, the prime minister," according to *The Sunday Times*, October 25, 1998, "that a newly formed Jewish underground may try to bomb Muslim holy shrines or assassinate Arab and Israeli leaders in an effort to stop troops withdrawing from the West Bank."

President Clinton who faces impeachment hearings, and the Democratic party facing elections today, are the clear winners. Israel's security concerns have been addressed, without addressing the security concerns of Palestinians, and any delay helps Israel establish facts on the ground which may predetermine the final outcome of the peace process.

An Israeli investigative commission found Sharon, then defense minister, responsible for the 1982 massacre by Lebanese Christian militia of about 900 men, women, and children at the Sabra and Shatila refugee camps following Israel's invasion of Lebanon, and the withdrawal of Palestinian guerrilla forces from the city. At the Wye River Plantation meeting last month, Sharon ignored Arafat's salute.

November 11, 1998

Israel's Willing Executioners

While Israel manufactures weapons of mass destruction, occupies land by force for over 30 years, and has been condemned by the UN Security Council and General Assembly in several dozen resolutions, Israel's willing executioners are preparing to bomb Iraq, and to put Americans unnecessarily at risk.

"Israel has repeatedly accused Arab and Islamic countries hostile to it of manufacturing [weapons of mass destruction] on a large scale," says the *Times* of London (September 25), "but has never admitted possessing biological or chemical weapons, just as it has never owned up to a nuclear capability, although it is an open secret that the country has at least 200 nuclear warheads."

For over 30 years Israel has illegally occupied portions of the West Bank, Gaza, Lebanon, and Syria. UN Security Council Resolution 242, passed November 22, 1967, emphasized "the inadmissibility of the acquisition of territory by war," and contained the underlying formula for all Middle East peace initiatives since then—land for peace. During this period Israel has brutalized the Palestinians, instigated the massacre of refugees in Lebanon, and bombed the UN supervised refugee camp at Qana. Palestinians have retaliated with suicide bombings.

Iraqi charges of UNSCOM—the organization charged with finding Iraq's weapons of mass destruction—being a U.S.-Israel operation cannot be dismissed.

"According to three officials with direct knowledge of the relationship," says the *Washington Post* (September 29), "Israel had become by July 1995 the most important single contributor among the dozens of UN member states that have supplied information to UNSCOM since its creation in April 1991....Israel and UNSCOM have protected the operation among their most sensitive secrets."

BBC News Online reported (November 3) that a British Member of Parliament has said that "four members of the United Nations weapons inspection team in Iraq are Israeli spies. Labour's George Galloway, who has campaigned against air strikes on Iraq, named four people he alleged were agents of Mossad, the Israeli secret service, working under false names and papers with the UNSCOM team."

Peter J. Boyer's article in *The New Yorker* (November 9) confirms that UNSCOM inspector Scott Ritter began exchanging information with Israeli intelligence in 1994. Ritter provided Israel U-2 spy plane photos, which could be used to target Iraq, and Ritter's inspections were guided by Israel.

Brian Jenkins of CNBC reported (November 11) that NBC has confirmed through their own sources that UNSCOM inspectors have indeed been providing intelligence information, including targeting intelligence information, to the U.S. government.

Meanwhile, sanctions imposed after the 1991 Gulf War have devastated the Iraqi people. According to the International Action Center, "The sanctions have already killed 1.5 million Iraqis over the past eight years. 8,000 more die each month. Sanctions are genocidal weapons of mass destruction and they must be lifted immediately. The weapons inspection process proved itself to be an endless farce. It is incredibly hypocritical for the U.S.—with more weapons than all other countries combined—to be leading the way."

With no end to UN sanctions in sight, Iraq halted cooperation with UN weapons inspectors on October 31, but said it wants a peaceful solution, and has permitted the International Atomic Energy Agency, accompanied by UNSCOM inspectors, to continue inspections unimpeded. Iraq says it has destroyed its weapons of mass destruction, and that "it is the U.S. that is not complying with UN resolutions."

President Clinton chose the anniversary of the armistice ending World War I to further threaten Iraq. He charges that failure to act "would permanently damage the credibility of the UN Security Council to act as a force for promoting international peace." It is a phrase reminiscent of Plato's unnamed Athenian Stranger who favored "seeking peace by making war," says former U.S. Attorney General Ramsey Clark. Defense Secretary William S. Cohen warned that U.S. credibility is on the line, and "time is running out for Iraq to avert a military strike."

To understand the U.S. rush to war one has only to look as far as those advising President Clinton. While Arabs and Muslims are excluded from high-level policy making, "Jewish Americans," says Graham E. Fuller, former vice-chairman of the National Intelligence Council at the CIA, "occupy nearly every single senior position relating to U.S. Arab-Israeli policy." One might say the same about U.S. media. Israel is leading the U.S. to war, and Americans may die protecting Israel's hegemony over the Middle East.

President Clinton is known for his close ties to the American Israel Public Affairs Committee. "AIPAC's former president, David Steiner, resigned in the fall of 1992," wrote the *Washington Report on Middle East Affairs* (February/March 1994), "after publication of a tape recording in which he was heard boasting that he was 'negotiating' with the Clinton campaign over who would be the new administration's secretary of state."

The UN lost credibility during the Gulf War when it hastily passed Resolution 678 authorizing the use of force against Iraq, but failed to prevent Serb massacres in Bosnia and Kosova. President Clinton's credibility has, to put it charitably, been severely compromised. What is on the line now are American lives, and American values. Israel's willing executioners are sacrificing both, as they lead us to the genocide of a decimated people.

["United States officials said on Wednesday that American spies had worked undercover on teams of United Nations arms inspectors ferreting out secret Iraqi weapons programs."—Tim Weiner, "U.S. Spied on Iraq Under UN Cover, Officials Now Say," *New York Times*, January 7, 1999]

["Israel and the United States signed agreements today that will give Israeli scientists access to some types of U.S. nuclear technology. The access had previously been denied because Israel refuses to sign the 1968 Nuclear Nonproliferation Treaty."— "United States to Allow Israeli Scientists Access to Nuclear Technology," *ABC News*, February 2, 2000]

November 16, 1998

President Clinton Misrepresented Iraq Threat

No evidence UNSCOM found any WMD since 1991

Did President Clinton misrepresent the threat from Iraq's alleged weapons of mass destruction? Like the "Iraq crisis" in February, we believe this "crisis" too was a sham.

Syndicated columnist Robert D. Novak apparently supports our conclusion. The following are excerpts from "One-Man Show on Iraq" by Robert D. Novak (*Washington Post,* November 16, 1998, Op-Ed page):

"[Lawmakers] could ask angry Pentagon staff officers why the J-3 operations section started logistical prepositioning a month ago— before Saddam Hussein on October 31 triggered the new crisis by restricting inspectors."

"Since UNSCOM (the United Nations inspecting organization) never has on its own been able to find chemical or germ weapons of mass destruction in Iraq, how can Saddam Hussein's denial of inspection rights be considered so grave a threat to U.S. security as to enable Clinton as commander in chief to exercise inherent constitutional powers?"

Former congressman, and presidential candidate, Jack Kemp said last week that "his staff can find no evidence of UNSCOM documentation of further weapons finds." Adds Kemp, "Indeed, when I asked Rubin about this on Friday, he cited specifically only the weapons pointed out by the Iraqis in 1991, though he added that he had been assured there have been other discoveries."

Peter J. Boyer's article (*The New Yorker,* November 9) gives credence to widely discounted claims Thursday by Iraqi Deputy Prime Minister Tariq Aziz that UNSCOM worked closely with the CIA and the Israeli Mossad.

One Pentagon staffer, writes Mr. Novak, "suspects that the timing of Clinton's response was purely political, designed to offset impeachment proceedings." Had the U.S. proceeded with the bombing of Iraq, aborted 18 minutes before the scheduled launch, the Pentagon estimates that 10,000 Iraqis would have been killed.

November 17, 1998

Wye Not Peace: Accords Dead on Arrival

The Wye River Accords announced October 23, 1998 were dead on arrival, and are more likely to lead to continued strife, and perhaps civil war, rather than to peace.

Amidst the hoopla surrounding the White House announcement by President Clinton, and the Chairman Arafat-President Netanyahu handshake, no mention was made of the basic dispute between the Palestinian Authority, and the State of Israel—statehood, borders, refugees, settlements, home demolitions, water rights, Jerusalem. Instead the announced accords require the Palestinian Authority to take measures aimed at guaranteeing the security of Israel, while Israel is not required to take any measures to guarantee the security of Palestinians.

With Arafat's self-imposed, May 4, 1999, deadline for the announcement of a Palestinian state fast approaching (May 4 being the date for completion of the peace process under the Oslo agreement), the accords seem aimed at placing more conditions on the Palestinians for return of territories occupied by Israel, and for giving Netanyahu an excuse to deny the return of those territories. They also require Arafat to take repressive measures guaranteed to increase divisions among Palestinians, and may even lead to civil war.

Under the October 23 accords, Chairman Arafat agreed to step up "antiterrorist efforts" in the West Bank, and to eliminate anti-Israel provisions in the PLO founding charter. The Israelis agreed to cede 13 percent more of the occupied territory on the West Bank, and release 750 of the 3,000 political prisoners held without trial in Israeli jails.

Arafat's "antiterrorist efforts," to be monitored by the U.S. Central Intelligence Agency, are intended to further crackdown on Palestinians opposed to the agreement. Arafat agreed to disarm about 10,000 of the PLO police force, stifle dissident voices, and to arrest Palestinians on the basis of "evidence" provided by Israel. In the days following the announced accords, Arafat's forces muzzled Sheikh Yassin, Hamas' spiritual leader, and arrested about 300 of the Hamas resistance.

The Wye River accords could hardly have been more fortuitous for President Clinton, and the Democratic Party. At the November 8 elections, rather than expected victories, the Republican Party lost ground, and President Clinton's chances for impeachment receded with the humbled Republican Party scrambling to find a way out of the impeachments hearings. "God, I'd like to forget all of this. I mean, who needs it?" said Judiciary Chairman Henry J. Hyde (R-Ill).

As for the Palestinians, the New York based Human Rights Watch has stated, "The history of the Israeli-Palestinian conflict is replete with serious human rights violations—arbitrary arrest, torture, and unfair trials—that the parties have tried to justify by invoking security concerns....Instead of creating strong mechanisms to prevent such violations, many sections of the Wye River [Accord] can be read as encouraging them.

According to the *Washington Post* (November 6), "In most of the Middle East the interim peace accord that emerged from the Wye Plantation talks last month has landed with a thud, eliciting caution, at best, and outright disdain among those who see the agreement as a betrayal of Palestinian aspirations to regain all of the West Bank lands occupied by Israel."

"The reaction in such hard-line states as Iran, Syria, and Libya has been characteristically harsh," says the *Washington Post*, and "has failed to spark much emotion or hope even in such moderate states as Egypt, a close ally of the United States and a staunch supporter of the peace process since it became the first Arab state to make peace with Israel in 1979."

"How much baksheesh did Clinton have to dish out?" asks Eric Margolis, *The Toronto Sun* (October 25), "President Jimmy Carter's much ballyhooed Camp David agreement was the biggest bribe in history. Israel got U.S. $3 billion and Egypt $800 million—annually. Additional sums were covertly paid to Sadat and his cronies. Israel got lots of secret goodies."

The predictable results of Arafat's surrender to United States' largess, and to the Israeli occupation force are evident.

Izzedine al Qassem brigades, Hamas' military arm, in a leaflet faxed to news organizations announced: "The (Palestinian) Authority's security apparatus, its officials and elements, will never be safe."

"Israel's internal security service has warned Benjamin Netanyahu," according to the *Sunday Times* (October 25), "that a newly formed Jewish underground may try to bomb Muslim holy shrines or assassinate Arab and Israeli leaders in an effort to stop troops withdrawing from the West Bank."

And in Israel and the occupied territories the killings go on. *Associated Press* reports:

October 26—Two Palestinians commandeer the car of a Jewish settler in the West Bank town of Hebron, kill him and dump his body by the side of the road. An elderly Palestinian farmer is bludgeoned to death near a Jewish settlement in the West Bank, and an Israeli suspect is arrested.

October 29—A suicide bomber drives a car rigged with explosives into an Israeli jeep escorting a school bus in the Gaza Strip. The assailant and a soldier are killed. Hamas claims responsibility.

November 6—Two suicide bombers drive a car packed with explosives into the Mahane Yehuda outdoor market in Jerusalem, killing themselves and injuring 21 Israelis. Hamas claims responsibility.

These incidents, as expected, have given Israel the excuse it needed to delay ratification of the Wye River accords, and to continue its policy of settlement expansion.

Netanyahu has said he will not move forward with implementing the Wye River Accords until the Palestinians do more to combat Islamic militants. According to *Associated Press* (November 11), "Netanyahu aides have also said that construction in the Jewish neighborhood of Har Homa in traditionally Arab East Jerusalem would begin in the near future."

BBC News Online reports (November 16) that Israel's Foreign Minister, Ariel Sharon, days before he was due to lead negotiations on the final status of the occupied territories, said in a speech to members of one of Israel's extreme right parties. "Everyone should take action, should run, should grab more hills,...We'll expand the area. Whatever is seized will be ours. Whatever isn't seized will end up in their hands."

Meanwhile, Netanyahu demands that Hamas' military wing, Izeddine al Qassam, and the military wing of Islamic Jihad be outlawed. The Palestinian Authority says it outlawed them in 1996. "As for Jerusalem," says Netanyahu, "I have old news for our Palestinian neighbors: Jerusalem was, is, and will be the capital of the state of Israel."

Associated Press reported (November 16) that Netanyahu "suspended a West Bank troop pullback Monday and demanded that Yasser Arafat retract threats to use force to bring about a Palestinian state." If Israel refuses to carry out the withdrawals on time, says Palestinian negotiator Hassan Asfour the agreement is "as good as dead."

[UN Security Council Resolution 242, passed November 22, 1967, emphasized "the inadmissibility of the acquisition of territory by war," and contained the underlying formula for all Middle East peace initiatives since then—land for peace. In exchange for withdrawing from Egyptian, Jordanian, and Syrian territory captured in the 1967 war, Israel was promised peace by the Arab states. This resolution is the basis for peace talks begun in Madrid, Spain, in 1991.]

December 12, 1998

Sir Syed's Vision For Education

[Speech given by author, at Aligarh Muslim University in India, during the inaugural session of the conference commemorating the centenary of the death of the university's founder—Sir Syed Ahmad Khan.]

Thank you Vice Chancellor Mahmood-ur-Rehman, honored guests, faculty, and students. While I am descended from Sir Syed, I cannot claim to be an expert on his life and vision. I can only surmise what his vision must have been for the Muslims of India.

I believe his vision would have been based upon the condition of Muslims of that time, his perceptions of where the world was headed, and his knowledge of history. Using these same considerations, one may surmise what priority Sir Syed would have given to education today.

Therefore, the question I would like to present is, what is the priority that education deserves? In other words, what priority should we as individuals, as a family, as a society, give to education?

History may shed light on this issue. Being an engineer by profession, my knowledge of history is limited. It was the Gulf War of 1991 that evoked my interest in history. My focus, because of the principal parties to the Gulf War, became Islam, the United States, and eventually the European colonization since 1492. I would like to share, very briefly, what I learned during the past seven years.

Let us begin with the spread of Islam.

When Prophet Muhammad died in 632, he was the effective leader of all of southern Arabia. By 711, the Arabs had swept completely across North Africa to the Atlantic Ocean. In less than 100 years, the Bedouin tribesmen, inspired by the word of the Prophet, had carved out an empire stretching from the borders of India to the Atlantic Ocean—the largest empire that the world had yet seen.

Some have said this empire was carved out by the sword. Swords, while used by Muslim armies, cannot account for the spread of Islam. One example is sufficient to challenge the thesis that Islam was spread by the sword—Indonesia.

Indonesia is the largest Muslim country, with its people living on about 6,000 islands spread over a distance of about 5,000 kilometers. No Muslim armies landed in Indonesia. Islam spread across Indonesia with the example of Muslim traders.

What was the message these traders offered that led to Islam's rapid spread?

Simply put, the message was there is One God, that mankind is one, that goodness is the only measure of a person's worth. Man was urged to care for the poor, the infirm, the orphan, to respect all faiths, and to search for knowledge. The Quran is very clear about the Unity of mankind and respect for all faiths.

> For each we have appointed a divine law and traced out the way. Had Allah willed He could have made you one community. But that He may try you by that which He hath given you He made you as ye are. So vie one with another in good works. Unto Allah you will all return, and will then inform you of that wherein you differ.—(5:48)

Maulana Abul Kalam Azad, a leader of India's independence movement, twice president of the Indian National Congress, renowned scholar, and India's first education minister, said,

> The unity of man is the primary aim of religion. The message which every prophet delivered was that mankind were in reality one people and one community, and that there was but one god for all of them, and on that account they should serve Him to-

gether and live as members of one family. Such was the message which every religion delivered. But curiously, the followers of each religion discarded the message, so much so, that every country, every community and every race resolved itself into a separate entity and raised groupism to the position of religion.

The Quran is replete with verses inviting man to use his intellect, to ponder, to think and to know, for the goal of human life is to discover the Truth. Prophet Muhammad tells us, "The first thing created by god was the Intellect." And he also says, "One learned man is harder on the devil than a thousand ignorant worshippers." His words exhort us to, "Go in quest of knowledge even into China," and to, "Seek knowledge from the cradle to the grave." And where did the search for knowledge lead Muslims?

Islam gave the world its first true democracy.

M. N. Masud, private secretary to Maulana Azad, UNESCO mission chief to Indonesia, ambassador to Saudi Arabia writes in *Understanding Islam:*

> If true democracy is not confined to the form or model of government but is the way of life of a people wherein man is treated with respect and given dignity, irrespective of what he is or what he is not, then Islamic society, from the very birth of Islam, has been nearest to the ideal, much nearer to it than has been, perhaps, any other society in the recorded history of man.

I'm sure that Western audiences would immediately challenge this assertion. They may say that Greece was the first democracy. Not true. Greece was an oligarchy (where a few ruled the many). Slaves had no voice in their society, and neither did women.

Other Western audiences may point to the United States and its Declaration of Independence of 1776. But the U.S. too was an oligarchy. Native Americans, slaves, women, white men without property, had no voting rights. There are respected American writers who say that the U.S. is an oligarchy even today.

Islam was responsible for numerous advances in science, mathematics, medicine, liberal arts, and for Europe's renaissance.

The Muslims founded many centers of learning. Europeans flocked to Spain to study under Muslim scholars. Arabic was the language of Jewish, Christian and Muslim scholars in Europe until the fall of Muslim Spain in 1492.

His Royal Highness, The Prince of Wales, in a major speech titled "Islam and the West," said:

> Not only did Muslim Spain gather and preserve the intellectual content of ancient Greek and Roman civilization, it also interpreted and expanded upon that civilization, and made a vital contribution of its own in so many fields of human endeavour—in science, astronomy, mathematics, algebra (itself an Arabic word), law, history, medicine, pharmacology, optics, agriculture, architecture, theology, music.
>
> Cordoba in the 10th century was by far the most civilized city of Europe....Many of the traits on which Europe prides itself came to it from Muslim Spain. Diplomacy, free trade, open borders, the techniques of academic research, of anthropology, etiquette, fashion, alternative medicine, hospitals, all came from this great city of cities. Mediaeval Islam was a religion of remarkable tolerance for its time, allowing Jews and Christians to practice their inherited beliefs, and setting an example which was not, unfortunately, copied for many centuries in the West.
>
> [Islam] has contributed so much towards the civilization which we all too often think of, wrongly, as entirely Western. Islam is part of our past and present, in all fields of human endeavour. It has helped to create modern Europe. It is part of our own inheritance, not a thing apart.

How did the Muslims accomplish this, and what does this say about the priority these Muslims gave to education?

Perhaps the answer lies in Will Durant's *Story of Civilization* (vol. IV, p. 237). Mr. Durant writes:

> When Baghdad was destroyed by the Mongols it had thirty-six public libraries. Private libraries were numberless. It was a fashion among the rich to have an ample collection of books. A physician refused the invitation of the Sultan of Bokhara to come and live at his court, on the ground that he would need 400 camels to transport his library. Al-Waqidi, dying, left 600 boxes of books, each box so heavy that two men were needed to carry it. Princes like Sahab ibn Abbas in the 10th century might own as many books as could be found in all the libraries of Europe combined.

These words of Will Durant say a lot about Muslims' thirst for knowledge at the time that Islam was at its zenith. I believe, also, these words say a lot about the priority Sir Syed must have given to education. We as individuals, as a family, as a society, should do no less.

["When his contemporaries heard the words islam and muslim, they understood them as denoting man's 'self-surrender to God' and 'one who surrenders himself to God,' without limiting himself to any specific community or denomination—e.g., in 3:67, where Abraham is spoken of as having 'surrendered himself unto God' (kana musliman), or in 3:52 where the disciples of Jesus say, 'Bear thou witness that we have surrendered ourselves unto God (bianna musliman)." In Arabic, this original meaning has remained unimpaired, and no Arab scholar has ever become oblivious of the wide connotation of these terms. Not so, however, the non-Arab of our day, believer and nonbeliever alike: to him, islam and muslim usually bear a restricted, historically circumscribed significance, and apply exclusively to the followers of the Prophet Muhammad—Muhammad Asad, *The Message of the Quran*, p. vi]

December 18, 1998

Polls as Predictable as Hitler's Willing Executioners

Poll results showing the American public solidly behind the U.S. bombing of Iraq reveal nothing more than the effectiveness of the propaganda war against Saddam Hussein, Arabs, Muslims, and Islam.

After years of biased media coverage of events relating to Arabs and Muslims, how else is the American public to react?

Thoughtful voices opposed to U.S. imperial policies are seldom heard. How often are persons like former U.S. Attorney General Ramsey Clark, professor and prolific writer Noam Chomsky, historian Howard Zinn, or informed journalists like Robert Fisk asked to appear on major TV news or talk shows? How often do we see lawyers on network TV arguing the fine points of law relating to U.S. foreign affairs like they do in the domestic affairs of O.J. Simpson, Monica Lewinsky, and President Clinton?

Self-serving media critics fail to inform the public, or chastise the media, when elementary rules of journalism are not followed.

Is it not relevant when one writes about Iraq's weapons of mass destruction, to mention neighboring Israel's? Is it not relevant when one writes of Iraq's violation of UN resolutions to mention Israel's? Is it not relevant when one writes of Iraq's use of chemical or biological weapons to mention Israel's, Britain's, and ours?

Would the poll results be any different if Americans were told that the U.S. invasion of Panama to seize President Noriega (itself a violation of international law) resulted in about ten times as many deaths as did Iraq's invasion of Kuwait?

After years of biased media coverage, the results of polls regarding the U.S. bombing of Iraq are as predictable as those of a lynch mob, or of Hitler's willing executioners.

December 22, 1998

Clinton Manufactured Crisis, Violated Constitution

President Clinton, in launching the massive December 16 attack on Iraq, used a manufactured crisis to deceive the American people, and to bypass Congress' power to declare war.

Warplanes aboard the USS Enterprise, combined with more than 200 cruise missiles from eight Navy warships, converged on Iraqi targets at 5:06 P.M. EST (1:06 A.M. Baghdad time). Over a four-day period, reports U.S. Marine Gen. Anthony Zinni, who oversaw the Iraq attack, 300 strike fighters, bombers and support aircraft flew 600 sorties, more than half of them at night. Another 40 ships took part in the attack, with 10 of them firing cruise missiles. More than 600 bombs were dropped, 90 cruise missiles fired from the air and another 300 from ships at sea.

The United Nations Special Commission (UNSCOM) report Mr. Clinton used as cause for war, says syndicated columnist Robert D. Novak ("Wag the Congress," *Washington Post*, December 21), contains six complaints cited by Richard Butler, executive chairman of UNSCOM. These complaints "reflect Saddam Hussein's obnoxious style but do not compare to more than 400 unimpeded inspections reported by Iraq since cooperation resumed November 14."

Mr. Novak provides an example of the type of incidents Mr. Clinton used to justify the attack on Iraq. "On December 9 weapons inspectors from UNSCOM, acting on a tip, showed up without notification at the Baghdad headquarters of the ruling Baath Party to search for ballistic missile components. The Iraqi escorts, citing a 1996 agreement, said only four inspectors could enter."

The Butler report itself was a setup.

According to Rowan Scarborough of the *Washington Times* ("Did White House orchestrate a crisis?" December 18), Scott Ritter, a former UN inspector, said Mr. Butler conferred with the Clinton administration's national security staff on how to write his report of noncompliance before submitting it to the UN Security Council. The former inspector said the White House wanted to ensure the report contained sufficiently tough language on which to justify its decision to bomb Iraq. "I'm telling you this was a preordained conclusion. This inspection was a total setup by the United States," said Ritter. Mr. Ritter resigned from UNSCOM in August, accusing the Clinton administration of interfering in how and when inspections were carried out.

The decision to attack Iraq was made before the Bultler report was submitted to the UN Security Council.

The MacLaughlin Group (NBC, December 18) reported that while the president told the nation Wednesday night that the attack was triggered by this Butler report, the "time line into the bombing itself shows that the president ordered airstrikes 48 hours before he saw the report."

Mr. Clinton's reference to Iraq's nuclear weapons was completely at odds with the report of the agency charged with reporting on Iraq's clandestine nuclear weapons capabilities.

The MacLaughlin Group reported that there is another report that was filed with the UNSCOM report: the International Atomic Energy Agency report. The IAEA worked hand in glove with UNSCOM. The agency is charged with determining any Iraqi clandestine nuclear weapons capabilities. This week the IAEA filed a companion separate report, accompanying the UNSCOM report, that went largely unnoticed. In it, the IAEA gives Iraq a clean nuclear bill of health, describing Iraq's level of cooperation as, "efficient and effective."

President Clinton told another lie, says Howard Zinn, professor emeritus of history at Boston University, and author of the bestselling *A People's History of the United Sates*. Mr. Clinton said that other nations besides Iraq have weapons of mass destruction, but Iraq alone has used them. Says Prof. Zinn, "He could only say this to a population deprived of history. The United States has supplied Turkey, Israel, and Indonesia with such weapons, and they have used them against civilian populations. But the nation most guilty is our own. No nation in the world possesses greater weapons of mass destruction than we do, and none has used them more often, or with greater loss of civilian life. In Hiroshima hundreds of thousands died, in Korea and Vietnam millions died as a result of our use of such weapons."

Mr. Zinn's words echo those of Rev. Martin Luther King, Jr., cited by former U.S. Attorney General Ramsey Clark, in a December 20 letter sent to each member of the Security Council. Said Rev. King, "The greatest purveyor of violence on earth is my own government."

Presidential candidate Patrick J. Buchanan ("Failed President, Flawed Policy," December 18) says, "It is time to ask how grave a threat Iraq is to America. In the Gulf War, Iraq did not attack us; we attacked Iraq. We launched the 'round-the-clock air strikes with 2,000 planes for six weeks; Iraq fired back a handful of scuds. Iraq killed scores of Americans; we killed thousands of Iraqis. Yes, Saddam makes 'war on his own people,' but who inflicts the greater suffering—Saddam or a U.S.-led embargo that has claimed the lives of 239,000 children, 5 years old and under, since 1990?"

Presidential candidate Jack Kemp, in a December 18 letter to U.S. Senate Majority Leader Trent Lott said that "reports coming out of the Pentagon and from a former UN weapons inspector raise a number of serious and troubling questions that, in my opinion, vindicate your skepticism. These questions are so troubling that I believe they warrant immediate congressional inquiries."

Matthew Rothschild, editor of the *Progressive Magazine*, writes ("An Attack That Makes No Sense," *Los Angeles Times*, December 17, 1998), "The U.S. bombing campaign against Iraq is an act of war not sanctioned by international law or by the U.S. Constitution. Within 72 hours of his grand jury appearance in August, Clinton bombed Sudan and Afghanistan. Now, the day before he faced impeachment, he attacks Baghdad and other locations in Iraq. Our founders gave Congress the sole power to declare war. Congress has not issued such a declaration in this instance. According to international law, a country can take unilateral action against another country only for the purpose of self-defense. But this bombing attack can hardly be called an act of self-defense. Saddam has not attacked the United States and does not pose an imminent threat to us."

Two congressmen have broken ranks with the U.S. Congress to speak out against Mr. Clinton's attack on Iraq, and his usurpation of Congress' power.

Last Wednesday, Rep. Ron Paul (R-TX) called on President Clinton to resign for the good of the country and the safety of American soldiers. "Once again President Clinton is using American troops to deflect attention from his record of lies, distortions, obstruction of justice and abuse of power. Just a couple of months ago, the President launched an attack against the nation of Sudan in an attempt to cover over his personal problems; an attack which we know now had no basis whatsoever in protecting U.S. interests."

In a little-noticed speech on the House floor last Thursday, Rep. David Skaggs (D-CO) said, "President Clinton acted in violation of the Constitution in ordering these attacks without authority of Congress."

January 18, 1999

Defense Increase Jeopardizes Social Security, Medicare

"Islamic terrorism" helps justify defense spending

Desperate to fend off the Republican-led impeachment process, President Clinton has agreed to an $124 billion increase in defense spending over seven years, thereby, jeopardizing his earlier commitments to education, social security, medicare, and programs for the poor.

Measured in 1995 dollars, U.S. defense spending has declined from a Cold War high of around $375 billion in 1988 to around $265 billion in 1997, according to the Stockholm International Peace Research Institute (SIPRI). Defense spending for the U.S.S.R. was around $260 billion in 1988. With the break up of the U.S.S.R., Russia's defense spending has declined to around $30 billion annually. Nevertheless,

U.S. military leaders warned that funds were needed to fill alarming gaps in military readiness.

"The scope of the problem was driven home," writes Bradley Graham (*Washington Post*, January 14), after Clinton "listened to generals and admirals cite mounting pilot shortages, ships cruising without full crews, rising cannibalization of parts from inactive weapons to make active ones and cutbacks in army training."

Others remain unconvinced of the need for defense spending increases.

"Here we go again," says Rear Admiral Eugene Carroll, USN (Ret.), Deputy Director at the Center for Defense Information, "The U.S. already spends substantially more for military forces than any other nation, with no significant threats to our national security. We're engaged in an arms race with ourselves."

"Americans don't need to spend more money for military security," says Admiral Carroll. "What we should do is to quit wasting money on forces and weapons we don't need to fight nonexistent enemies abroad. Instead, we ought to use the same dollars to address pressing national needs such as improved education, medical care, housing and law enforcement right here at home."

Former U.S. presidential candidate Patrick J. Buchanan, writing in *The American Cause* (January 12) asks, "With the Cold War over, why invite terrorist attacks on our citizens and country, ultimately with biological, chemical or nuclear weapons? No nation threatens us."

Mr. Buchanan cites a paper by the Cato Institute's Ivan Eland, "Does U.S. Intervention Overseas Breed Terrorism? The Historical Record," which documents how attacks on the U.S., or on U.S. citizens, were a direct result of U.S. intervention. Mr. Buchanan's examples include Pearl Harbor, Viet Nam, Palestine, Lebanon, Libya, Iran, Somalia, and Saudi Arabia.

Says Mr. Buchanan, "America is the only nation on Earth to claim a right to intervene militarily in every region of the world. But this foreign policy is not America's tradition; it is an aberration. During our first 150 years, we renounced interventionism and threatened war on any foreign power that dared to intervene in our hemisphere."

But the Pentagon has resisted budget cuts for a decade.

Former U.S. Defense Secretary Robert S. McNamara, and Lawrence J. Korb, an assistant secretary of defense during the Reagan administration, in their December 11, 1989 testimony before the Senate Budget Committee, stated that U.S. defense spending could safely be cut in half over the next five years.

Anxious to protect cold war levels of defense spending, the Pentagon manufactured the threat of Islamic fundamentalism (Leon T. Hadar, "The Green Peril: Creating the Islamic Fundamentalist Threat"), rogue states and nuclear outlaws (Michael Klare, *Rogue States and Nuclear Outlaws*).

While Russia's defense spending declined to about 15 percent of Cold War levels, U.S. defense spending declined to about the 70 percent level. The accompanying chart, based on information from SIPRI, shows annual defense spending in billions (1995 $) for the U.S., its allies, and potential adversaries.

The total defense spending of all the "rogue states," Cuba, Iran, Iraq, Libya, North Korea and Syria, remains at about $15 billion annually. Iran and Iraq spent only $3.3 billion and $1.2 billion respectively in 1996.

Defense Spending (Billions 1995 $)

	US/Allies	US	Allies	Russia	China/India	Rogues
1988	527	380	147	260	13	15
1989	523	375	148	240	14	15
1990	518	370	148	200	14	15
1991	468	320	148	125	14	15
1992	473	335	138	50	14	15
1993	458	325	133	48	15	15
1994	431	300	131	45	16	15
1995	406	280	126	40	16	15
1996	395	270	125	40	16	15
1997	387	265	122	40	17	15

The total defense spending of Russia, China, and India is about 50 percent that of U.S. allies—the United Kingdom, Germany, and France—and less than 15 percent that of the U.S. plus its allies.

Scaling back defense spending, and restructuring U.S. spending to better meet the needs of the new millennium, a daunting task for any president, was within Mr. Clinton's grasp. But this immensely popular Democratic president, crippled by his private behavior, caved in to the Pentagon. Mr. Clinton squandered, what may have been his last chance, to leave a positive mark on history.

William Hartung, senior fellow of the World Policy Institute, claims that "a Monica-weakened Clinton bowed last fall to the Pentagon's demands for more funding" (*Milwaukee Sentinel & Journal,* January 11). Mr. Hartung contends that "the arms industry has launched a concerted lobbying campaign aimed at increasing military spending and arms exports. These initiatives are driven by profit and pork barrel politics, not by the objective assessment of how best to defend the United States in a post-cold war period."

Mr. Clinton, having cut welfare spending by $55 billion over six years in 1996, is giving defense an $124 billion spending increase. The surplus which was to have been targeted for education, Social Security, Medicare, and for the poor will be used to fight U.S. provoked "terrorism."

Having bombed a pharmaceutical factory in Sudan and huts in Afghanistan to divert attention from Monica Lewinsky's testimony before the grand jury, having "flattened an agricultural school, damaged at least a dozen other schools and hospitals and knocked out water supplies for 300,000 people in Baghdad" (*Reuters,* January 6) at the start of the impeachment process, Mr. Clinton has now jeopardized the needs of the poor, the infirm, and the middle class, to woo the Republicans during his trial in the U.S. Senate.

["Under Boris Yeltsin, conventional forces bore the brunt of downsizing and shrinking budgets. Priority was given to the strategic nuclear force, which today is Russia's only real claim to status as a military power. Russia still has a standing force of 1.5 million troops, slightly larger than the one maintained by the United States, but the budget will be only $4 billion this year, compared with the Pentagon's $284 billion."—Steven Lee Myers, "Russia Fights Stalinist Battles With American Tactics," *New York Times,* January 16, 2000]

["A privately launched spy satellite has revealed what American Intelligence has kept secret for years—that North Korea's only operational missile test centre is a primitive facility consisting of a 'shed, a dirt road, a launch pad and a rice paddy.' Missile experts in the United States dismissed Washington's fears that the rogue nation now posed a serious threat to America's security."—Michael Evans, "Spy Pictures Show Korea's Empty Threat," *Times,* January 12, 2000]

February 15, 1999

Rogue State Par Excellence

By any objective criteria, based upon generally accepted norms for civil society, the rogue state par excellence is not among the frequently cited group of states—Cuba, Libya, Iran, Iraq, North Korea, and Syria.

The rogue state par excellence has carried on a campaign of international terrorism and genocide, has refused to abide by international law or treaties, has violated norms of civil society, and has defied world opinion to a degree unmatched by the frequently cited "rogue states." Some recent examples:

August 20, 1998—After two embassies, in Nairobi and Dar es Salaam, had been blown up, this rogue state launched a missile strike on the El Shifa pharmaceutical factory in Sudan, thereby, destroying more than 50 percent of this impoverished nations' medicine producing capability. Today the London-based *Independent* reports that an investigation of the missile attack by Kroll Associates has concluded that there was no evidence to link the facility or its owner to international terrorism.

August 20, 1998—This rogue state fired 75 cruise missiles into the east of Afghanistan. The missile strike was described as a blow at Osama bin Laden's camp for training terrorists. A few huts were destroyed, and several civilians killed or injured.

December 16, 1998—On the pretext that Iraq was not cooperating with the United Nations Special Commission, this rogue state launched a massive attack on Iraq. Over a four-day period 300 strike fighters, bombers and support aircraft flew 600 sorties, more than half of them at night. Another 40 ships took part in the attack, with 10 of them firing cruise missiles. More than 600 bombs were dropped, 90 cruise missiles fired from the air and another 300 from ships at sea.

These attacks, in which this rogue state acted as judge, jury, and executioner, violated the United Nations charter, and Security Council resolutions. They were almost universally condemned.

Using its $265 billion per year military machine, its economic power, and $97 million appropriated for the purpose of toppling the Iraqi government, this rogue state has maintained crippling sanctions on Iraq whose military outlays were $3 billion annually at their peak, and about $1.2 billion recently. According to UNICEF statistics cited by Dennis Halliday, the United Nations Humanitarian Coordinator for Iraq who resigned in protest, these sanctions have been killing five or six thousand children every month since the 1991 Gulf War.

Also, as a result of at least one million rounds of ammunition, coated in a radioactive material known as depleted uranium, or DU, fired upon a retreating Iraqi army at the close of the Gulf War, three times more children are being born with congenital deformities than before the Gulf war reports the London-based *Guardian/Observer* (December 21, 1998). In both Britain and the United States, veterans of that same war are coming forward with reports of sick and dying children.

Since mid-January of this year, this rogue state has been dropping bombs on Iraqi radar and missile sites, none of which violate any law or treaty. Frequently, civilians are killed and injured. This is done under the guise of protecting dissident groups in Iraq. The "no fly zones" imposed upon Iraq by this rogue state and its allies have no basis in law or treaty, and are a flimsy cover for violating the airspace of a sovereign nation.

The *Washington Post* (December 22) reported last year that this rogue state announced its decision to use a commercial reactor for military nuclear programs. This breaks a 53-year nonproliferation policy it has long urged upon other countries, most recently North Korea, India and Iraq, not to use nuclear power reactors to produce plutonium or highly-enriched uranium, two other key components of nuclear bombs.

About a week ago, the *Associated Press* (February 10) reported that this rogue state conducted an underground nuclear test. It was the sixth such test by this rogue state since a 1992 global ban on test explosions of nuclear weapons.

This rogue state has violated the Chemical Weapons Convention since it was ratified (*Washington Post*, September 17). According to the Washington based Stimson Center, "For the past 18 months, the [rogue state] has been the malignancy in the midst of the CWC."

Now this rogue state proposes to violate the 1972 Antiballistic Missile Treaty. Its current budget proposal contains $6.6 billion for a national missile defense system using space-based sensors, and ground-based missiles, which experts believe won't work, but which is bound to accelerate the arms race.

While urging nonproliferation of weapons by others, this rogue state is the biggest exporter of weapons. According to the International Institute for Strategic Studies, global arms trade expanded by eight percent in real terms in 1996 to $39.9 billion. Most of this expansion was due to increased demand by East Asia and the Middle East. Forty-four percent of these exports, or $17 billion, were from this rogue state.

While championing democracy, this rogue state supports and sustains authoritarian regimes, and monarchies, against the wishes of their people. It brands those who fight for democracy, or independence from foreign domination, as terrorists.

Last week, this rogue state defied world opinion by voting against the UN General Assembly resolution calling for an international conference on July 15, 1999 on Israeli settlements in traditionally Arab areas that Palestinians claim are illegal. The vote was 115 to 2 with five abstentions.

While suing tobacco companies for damages due to smoking-related illnesses (in a deal reminiscent of the Opium Wars fought by Britain to force China to buy opium, and to settle for peace by giving away Hong Kong), this rogue state used the General Agreement on Tariffs and Trade to force Thailand into buying imported cigarettes which the Thai government feared would hinder their efforts to control smoking, and consequently smoking-related illnesses.

While bribery has become an acknowledged way of life in many countries, says renowned attorney Gerry Spence in *Give Me Liberty!*, in the U.S. "bribery, made legal, is yet more evil, permitting the corporate core to buy and own the [legislature] and the presidency with pious immunity."

While millions lack health care, and subsist at poverty levels, while thousands sleep on the street, this rogue state's "federal government alone shells out $125 billion a year in corporate welfare." ("Corporate Welfare," *TIME*, November 9, 1998, Special Report). This, in the midst of one of the more robust economic periods in it's history. "Indeed, thus far in the 1990's, corporate profits have totaled $4.5 trillion—a sum equal to the cumulative paychecks of 50 million working [citizens] who earned less than $25,000 a year, for eight years."

According to *Rights for All*, a 153 page report from Amnesty International, this rogue state has more prisoners known to be awaiting execution than any other country. Prisons for adults also hold at least 3,500 child convicts, in violation of an international convention on civil rights.

In this rogue state's prisons, says Amnesty International, "thousands of people are subjected to sustained and deliberate brutality at the hands of police officers. Cruel, degrading and sometimes life-threatening methods of restraint continue to be a feature of [its] criminal justice system."

Amnesty says that "inmates are physically and sexually abused by other inmates and by guards. Sanctions against those responsible for these abuses are rare. Prison guards restrain the inmates with electric shock stun guns, leg irons, pepper spray and restraint chairs. Some women prisoners have given birth while in shackles."

This rogue state, reports the *Washington Post* (November 6, 1998), "skirts—or sometimes flouts—norms of due process. The use of secret evidence to deport or exclude aliens who are accused of no crimes—particularly when combined with laws permitting their indefinite detention—remains the most egregious offense. All the more so since in some of these cases, the evidence—when it finally emerges—seems less than impressive."

"The rise in counterterrorism wiretapping and physical searching under the Foreign Intelligence Surveillance Act," says the *Washington Post*, "also presents difficulties, as do asset forfeiture proceedings against people who are accused of supporting terrorist groups but have not been charged with crimes."

This rogue state spies on its citizens. The ECHELON system developed by this rogue state, in partnership with the Government Communications Headquarters (GCHQ) in Britain, the Communications Security Establishment (CSE) in Canada, and the Defense Signals Directorate (DSD) in Australia, is used to intercept ordinary e-mail, fax, telex, and telephone communications carried over the world's telecommunications networks.

Unlike many of the electronic spy systems developed during the

Cold War, says a report prepared for the European Parliament (*An Appraisal of Technologies of Political Control*), ECHELON is designed primarily for nonmilitary targets: governments, organizations, businesses, and individuals in virtually every country. It potentially affects every person communicating between (and sometimes within) countries anywhere in the world.

These are just a few examples of this rogue state's campaign of international terrorism and genocide, its refusal to abide by international law or treaties, and its violation of the norms of civil society—the very same allegations it makes against Cuba, Libya, Iran, Iraq, North Korea, and Syria.

This rogue state has been able to do all this because its major media either remain silent, or participate in deceiving its citizens, whereby, the vast majority of them remain uninformed. The concerned, informed minority is denied access to the primary channels of communication.

Let's face the facts. During the final decade of this millennium, by any objective criteria based upon generally accepted norms for civil society. The rogue state par excellence has been, and is, the United States—proclaimer of the right of all to "life, liberty, and the pursuit of happiness."

[For background read: William Blum, *Rogue State: A Guide to the World's Only Superpower*, Michael Klare, *Rogue States and Nuclear Outlaws*, and Howard Zinn, *Declarations of Independence: Cross-Examining American Ideology*.]

[See *Foreign Affairs*, March/April 1999, "The Lonely Superpower." "While the U.S. regularly denounces various countries as "rogue states," in the eyes of many countries it is becoming the rogue superpower."—Samuel P. Huntington]

[Also see *Foreign Affairs*, March/April 1999, Gary Wills, "Bully of the World"]

["Spy agencies in Britain and America eavesdropped on Diana, Princess of Wales and Mark Thatcher,...as part of a global system of monitoring communications, according to former intelligence officials."—Nick Fielding and Duncan Campbell, "Spy Agencies Listened in on Diana," *Sunday Times*, February 27, 2000]

["Russia today published a revised national security doctrine that reflects a growing sense of apprehension in the military and political establishment about Western intentions, especially after the NATO attack on Yugoslavia last year and amid continuing disagreements over Chechnya and arms control....The new document says nuclear weapons can be used 'in the case of the need to repulse an armed aggression, if all other methods of resolving the crisis situation are exhausted or have been ineffective.'"—David Hoffman, "New Russian Security Plan Criticizes West Doctrine Broadens Nuclear Use Policy," *Washington Post*, January 15, 2000]

March 27, 1999

Kosovo Bombing: Good Intentions, Bad Strategy?

After three days of NATO bombing, the Clinton administration has concluded that the situation in Kosovo has taken "a dramatic and serious turn for the worse." Critics of the bombing question its legality under U.S. and international law.

"Violence against civilians in Kosovo," reports Daniel Williams ("Reports Say Civilians Face Rising Violence," *Washington Post*, March 27), "appeared to be spiraling out of control today with reports of executions of ethnic Albanians [Kosovar Muslims] and the burning of houses, shops and cafes by masked and armed bands of Serbs who roamed the streets while residents cowered in their homes or fled in search of safety."

The Albanian government reported that Yugoslav forces had massacred 20 ethnic Albanian men after burning the villages of Goden, Prush and Zylfaj. Refugees fleeing Kosovo have reported to *Reuters* that "about 22,000 refugees were surrounded by Yugoslav forces in Cirez, a village in the central Drenica region."

Meanwhile, the numbers of refugees crossing into Macedonia has diminished from about 500 a day before the NATO airstrikes to about 300. Armed Serbs have begun to occupy the homes vacated by the Kosovar Muslims.

The legality of bombing Serbia, and its province Kosovo is being questioned both in the U.S. and abroad.

"I think it's unconstitutional," said Sen. Robert C. Smith (R-NH), a candidate for president, and opponent of the Clinton administration.

Russia and China have denounced the bombing as blatantly illegal. According to William Branigin and John M. Goshko ("Legality of Airstrikes Disputed in U.S., UN," *Washington Post*, March 27) , China called the airstrikes "a blatant aggression and act of vandalism" yesterday, and said, "the international community has a moral imperative to rise up against this barbarity." Russia said the attacks violate international law.

UN Secretary General Kofi Annan has pointed out that NATO explicitly acknowledges that the UN Security Council "has primary responsibility for maintaining international peace and security." UN members say the NATO attacks have not been authorized by any Security Council resolutions.

According to Peter Riddell ("Balkans Conflict: The Public Debate," *Times*, March 26), generally accepted legal doctrine has been, first, the supremacy of the United Nations Security Council over international disputes and authorizing the use of force; second, the right of countries to defend themselves; and, third, nonintervention in the internal disputes of sovereign states.

The *Economist* ("Stumbling into war," March 27) asks, "How would the West respond if one day, say, China were to carry out air strikes against an Indian government fighting to prevent its Muslim-majority province of Jammu & Kashmir from seceding?"

Legal issues aside, the NATO air campaign alone is neither likely to dislodge the Serb leader, Slobodan Milosevic, nor save the Kosovar Muslims. A ten-year embargo, and repeated bombing of Iraq, have not dislodged President Saddam Hussein.

Senior NATO and U.S. officials have begun to discuss the use of ground forces, which a divided U.S. Congress may oppose. The vote supporting U.S. participation in the NATO operation was 219 to 191 in the House, and 58 to 41 in the Senate.

Barring a change of heart by Mr. Milosevic, there seems to be no good way to avoid further bloodshed. The NATO bombing has worsened the situation for the Kosovar Muslims, and taken the world into new legal territory with unknown long-term repercussions.

Begun with good intentions, the NATO bombing may turn out to be bad strategy.

["Increasingly, it is suggested that NATO also should deploy ground troops. This is an option that President Clinton was wrong to rule out from the start, and he is wrong to rule it out now."—*Washington Post*, March 30, Editorial]

[General Klaus Naumann, chairman of NATO's Military Committee, said that the first phase of the strikes was made deliberately light, in the hope that President Slobodan Milosevic would concede quickly. He also accepted that the alliance was powerless to prevent the expulsion of the remaining ethnic Albanians.—*Independent*, May 5, 1999]

March 28, 1999

Kosovo Bombing: Bad Intentions, Good Strategy?

As NATO enters a fifth day of bombing raids on Serbia, with the declared aim of halting the slaughter of Kosovar Muslims, one has to ask what are NATO's real objectives? Is there a hidden agenda?

Wasn't the slaughter anticipated? Would a reasonable person attack while potential victims are held hostage? The U.S. did not attack Iraq's forces in Kuwait while Americans were held hostage during the Bush administration. The U.S. did not attack Iran while Americans were held hostage during the Carter administration.

Mr. Clinton, speaking from the White House four days ago, told reporters "Our purpose here is to prevent a humanitarian catastrophe. Our objective is to make it clear to Mr Milosevic he must choose peace, or we will limit his plans to make war." Whether this meant forcing the Yugoslav President to accept the peace accord negotiated at Rambouillet, and already accepted by representatives of Kosovo's Muslims, was not made clear.

Did U.S. and NATO planners not anticipate that if the Serbs were attacked more Muslims would be slaughtered? We have greater respect for U.S. and NATO military planners than to believe that they would launch air attacks, and not make provisions for minimizing the slaughter if that were really their mission. Notice how quickly the pilot of the $45 million, F-117 stealth fighter was rescued.

The Sunday Times reports ("NATO Attacks," March 28) that well before the NATO air strikes were launched President Clinton knew that "air strikes might provoke Serb soldiers into greater acts of butchery."

On March 15, says the *Sunday Times*, "Clinton and his cabinet members, including William Cohen, the defence secretary, and Sandy Berger, the national security adviser, sat in silence as Shelton [General Hugh Shelton, Chairman of the Joint Chiefs of Staff] outlined the thrust of the analysis. There was a danger, he told them, that far from helping to contain the savagery of the Serbs in Kosovo—a moral imperative cited by the president—air strikes might provoke Serb soldiers into greater acts of butchery. Air strikes alone, Shelton stated, could not stop Serb forces from executing Kosovars."

Perhaps, preventing a humanitarian catastrophe is not the mission.

Perhaps, the Kosovar Muslims are the sacrificial lambs; a cruel irony coinciding with *Eid-al Adha*. Perhaps, the NATO attack on a sovereign nation, the first in its 50-year history, is intended to justify NATO's continued existence, repeatedly questioned, since the disintegration of the U.S.S.R. which NATO was set up to defend against.

It is useful to recall what happened in Bosnia.

The Clinton plan for Bosnia, forged after the killing of 200,000 Muslims, in effect, legitimized Serb aggression. It set aside the Bosnian constitution, and forced the multiparty, secular, parliamentary democracy of Bosnia to accept a secession of 49 percent of its territory to the rebel Serbs. None of this would have been necessary were it not for the fact that the U.S.-led Western governments denied the Bosnian government that most basic of human rights—the right to self defense.

Today, as part of a 20,000 peacekeeping force, 6,000 U.S. troops are stationed in Bosnia, while thousands of Bosnian Muslims have been unable to return to their homes, and no senior Serb official has been tried for widely acknowledged war crimes. Serb warlords, General Ratko Mladic and Radovan Karadjic, continue to reside in Bosnia, in a district controlled by the very NATO troops now going to war with Serbia.

With 61 armed conflicts in progress around the world, why did NATO intervene in Serbia? The Russian slaughter of 80,000 Muslim civilians in Chechnya, in just two years, went on while NATO and the U.S. looked the other way. In fact, while this was happening the U.S. loaned hundreds of millions to Russia.

It is also useful to recall the legal status of Kosovo and Serbia.

According to the U.S. CIA *World Factbook*: "Serbia and Montenegro have asserted the formation of a joint independent state, but this entity has not been formally recognized as a state by the U.S.; the U.S. view is that the Socialist Federal Republic of Yugoslavia (SFRY), has dissolved and that none of the successor republics represents its continuation."

Professor of International Law, Francis A. Boyle, says, "the former Yugoslavia disintegrated as a state as the Badinter Commission found. As a result of this disintegration, the Kosovar people exercised their right of self-determination to establish the Kosova Republic in accordance with standard international law and practice." Prof. Boyle concedes that "world political circumstances do not yet seem ripe to obtain further international recognition of the Kosova Republic."

If American casualties were the concern, why weren't Muslim fighters asked to help save the Kosovar Muslims? Unconfirmed reports tell us many Muslims are ready and willing to help. Perhaps, rather than preventing a humanitarian catastrophe, the U.S.-led NATO bombing is a clever ruse to diminish dissent against U.S. pro-Israel policies, to strengthen U.S. puppet regimes in the Muslim world, or to grab the minerals and petroleum reserves of the Balkans?

Good intentions, bad strategy, or bad intentions, good strategy. Time will tell.

[“The sprawling state-owned Trepca mining complex, the most valuable piece of real estate in the Balkans, is worth at least $5 billion.”—Chris Hedges, "Below It All in Kosovo, A War's Glittering Prize," New York Times, July 8, 1998]

[“Kosovo also possesses 17 billion tons of coal reserves, and Kosovo (like Serbia and Albania) also has oil reserves.”—Barry Lituchy, "American Barbarism and the Big Lie Technique are the Winners in Kosovo," June 1999. Mr. Lituchy teaches history at Kingsborough Community College in New York.]

March 29, 1999

Clinton Forewarned, Precipitated Catastrophe

Europe's worst humanitarian disaster since World War II?

The *Sunday Times* of London reports that well before the NATO air strikes were launched President Clinton knew that "air strikes might provoke Serb soldiers into greater acts of butchery."

On March 15, reports the *Sunday Times* ("NATO Attacks," March 28), "Clinton and his cabinet members, including William Cohen, the defence secretary, and Sandy Berger, the national security adviser, sat in silence as Shelton [General Hugh Shelton, Chairman of the Joint Chiefs of Staff] outlined the thrust of the analysis. There was a danger, he told them, that far from helping to contain the savagery of the Serbs in

Kosovo—a moral imperative cited by the president—air strikes might provoke Serb soldiers into greater acts of butchery. Air strikes alone, Shelton stated, could not stop Serb forces from executing Kosovars."

Meanwhile, George Jahn of *Associated Press* reports ("NATO Races to Smash Serb Units," March 29), "Tens of thousands of ethnic Albanians streamed out of Kosovo today while NATO raced against time to smash Serb military units and ease what officials say is becoming Europe's worst humanitarian disaster since World War II."

According to *BBC News Online* ("Refugees Flee Kosovo Horror," March 29), the UN High Commissioner for Refugees believes that up to 25 percent of the population of Kosovo—more than 500,000 people—have fled their homes since the conflict began.

However, say Bill Sammon and Joyce Howard Price ("Pentagon Considers Ground Troops," *Washington Times*, March 29), "the White House yesterday repeated its assurance that President Clinton has no 'intention' of dispatching ground troops to Kosovo." There was no effective plan approved to prevent, or even minimize, the foreseeable humanitarian catastrophe.

Yet, speaking from the White House five days ago, President Clinton told reporters, "Our purpose here is to prevent a humanitarian catastrophe. Our objective is to make it clear to Mr Milosevic he must choose peace, or we will limit his plans to make war."

Our purpose here is to prevent a humanitarian catastrophe? Really, Mr. President?

["But launching a NATO air war against Milosevic was the triumph of threat over thought."—Bill Clinton's War, *The Progressive,* May 1999]

["She did not know that the A-10s that attacked her convoy (of Kosovar refugees) fired depleted uranium ammunition,...DU munitions may well be the cause of massive cancers in Iraq, and even of Gulf War Syndrome."—Robert Fisk, "Convoy of the Damned." *The Independent*, November 28, 1999]

["A year after NATO's intervention, the West's dream of Serbs and Albanians living together in Kosovo is dead."—Tom Walker, "West Abandons Dream of a Unified Kosovo," *Sunday Times*, February 13, 2000]

["But if Kosovo is not kept in one piece, as the Albanians have insisted and as the administration had pledged, the relations between NATO and the Albanian community will worsen, the officials said. 'The Albanians will feel we have betrayed them,' a senior NATO official said, 'and will turn against us.'"—Jane Perlez, "Spiral of Violence in Kosovo Divides U.S. and Its Allies," *New York Times*, March 12, 2000]

April 1, 1999

Clinton's Good Intentions Stymied by NATO, Congress?

Muslim nations conspicuous by their absence

Perhaps President Clinton never had a chance. He was damned if he did, and damned if he didn't.

If the U.S. had introduced ground troops, say Clinton aides, Clinton would have been criticized by the U.S. Congress for risking a military quagmire. Had he decided not to intervene at all in Kosovo, he would have been criticized for allowing NATO to standby in the face of a humanitarian disaster.

Therefore, despite warnings from General Hugh Shelton, Chairman of the Joint Chiefs of Staff, that "far from helping to contain the savagery of the Serbs in Kosovo—a moral imperative cited by the president—air strikes might provoke Serb soldiers into greater acts of butchery," the decision was made to go ahead with air strikes.

But that strategy is failing, and it appears that NATO is being timid in attacking Serbian command and control centers.

"Six days of intensive bombardment have failed to take out the Serb antiaircraft defences," report Andrew Marshall and Kim Sengupta ("War in the Balkans—Strategy may be failing, says NATO," *The Independent*, April 1), "with damage estimated at being only 'minimal to moderate,' say military sources. The hit rate is low, and the U.S. Air Force is down to its last hundred cruise missiles."

As for the sites hit one wonders why power plants, radio and television stations, and telephone exchanges were not targeted at the outset as they were in Iraq.

The Independent reports, "In the first five days of the campaign, about 90 attacks were made against at least 70 'individual sites.' Eight airfields had been targeted and seven aircraft destroyed in addition to four MiG-29s and a MiG-21 shot down while trying to intercept NATO planes. There have been 16 attacks on radar and early-warning systems and 16 attacks on surface-to-air missile sites. Twelve of the further 15 air defence facilities have also been struck."

President Clinton may have made matters worse for the Kosovars when, within two days of the first air strikes, he assured the American people that U.S. troops would only be sent into Kosovo in a peacekeeping role.

"How happy President Milosovic must have been to hear that," says Robert Fisk ("Lies, Deceit and Betrayal," *The Independent*, March 30). Fisk adds, "Already, Clinton was making excuses for NATO's air raids—and then promising that ground troops would never be sent to fight Serbian forces in Kosovo."

"So Milosevic's army pressed on eagerly. And when the next flood of Kosovars staggered into Macedonia with their stories of summary executions and house-burning, we were told yet again that things would have been worse without the air raids. Once NATO admitted that 500,000 Kosovars had been displaced, this lie was mercifully forgotten."

And throughout this humanitarian catastrophe, still unfolding, the leaders of Muslim countries have been conspicuous by their absence.

Clinton's aides would have us believe that President Clinton, with good intentions, at least tried to help the Kosovars. But somewhere along the way, perhaps stymied by NATO members' or U.S. Congress' opposition, or some hidden agenda, even the air strikes seemingly avoided key targets.

Given Mr. Clinton's record on Bosnia, Chechnya, Iraq, and Palestine, we remain skeptical. A more likely reason is that NATO was beginning to look like a paper tiger, and the U.S. couldn't have that just before NATO's 50th anniversary celebration on April 23 in Washington, D.C.

Now fewer good options (or the better of bad options) exist than before the NATO air strikes. But whatever strategy is now adopted, independence for Kosovo and swift justice for the aggressors should be high on the list of priorities.

In the meantime, the first priority should be to alleviate human suffering.

["The peacekeeping force is today 10,000 soldiers short of its authorized strength, ...Without clearer joint vision on Kosovo's future and bolder steps to counter Milosevic's subversion in the Balkans, NATO could still lose a war it claims to have won."—Jim Hoagland, "A Phony Peace," *Washington Post*, March 12, 2000]

April 7, 1999

Round One Milosevic, Will NATO Win War?

Serbian President Milosevic has won the first round. The issue now is will NATO persevere, or will Mr. Milosevic win the war?

About half the Kosovo population of 2 million has been uprooted since February 1998, and about 500,000 in the past two weeks since U.S. President Clinton told reporters, "Our purpose here is to prevent a humanitarian catastrophe."

Now the Macedonians, as NATO watches, are busy completing the ethnic cleansing begun by Mr. Milosevic. The Kosovars are being forcibly deported from the border camps to destinations not of their choosing.

"Under the cover of darkness on Monday night, 1,491 refugees were flown out of Skopje airport on 10 flights," reported Andrew Buncombe of *The Independent* today, and "all but one of which were heading for Turkey. When one refugee tried to run away he was frog-marched on board by security men. Yesterday morning another 600 refugees were flown out of the Macedonian capital—all bound for the same destination."

"No one would tell seven- year-old Ardita Berisha why she was being forced out of a country at gunpoint for the second time in a week," reported Daniel McGrory of the *Times*. Ardita "kept asking where they were going as an armed policeman shoved her into an airport bus, deporting the Berishas and 1,500 other confused refugees to Turkey yesterday."

"Rabia, her mother, began to cry and asked a security guard how her husband was meant to find them as he was stranded somewhere in Kosovo. The guard, his face partially covered by a surgical mask, shouted at her to do as she was told."

Mr. Milosevic has won the first round—ethnic cleansing. Rounds two (return of the Kosovars to their homes), three (independence for Kosovo), and four (bringing Mr. Milosevic to trial for war crimes) have yet to be fought, and Mr. Milosevic has just upped the ante.

Today, Yugoslavia sealed off Kosovo's main border crossings. "German Defense Minister Rudolf Scharping warned that the Yugoslavs may be planning to use the civilians in Kosovo as 'human shields' against NATO attack," reported George Jahn of *Associated Press*.

This is bound to complicate matters for NATO which has yet to commit the troops and weapons needed to help the Kosovars on the ground. And the forced deportation of the Kosovars to distant destinations will diminish the TV coverage which serves to mobilize public support for NATO action.

Will NATO persevere, or will rounds two, three, and four, also go to Mr. Milosevic? Despite the genuine concern of average citizens, the Kosovar Muslims have become a pawn in a deadly superpower game. NATO credibility, on the eve of its April 23 celebration of its 50th anniversary, is the prize.

May 7, 1999

U.S. Admits Mistake in Bombing Sudan

The Clinton administration will not challenge a lawsuit filed by a Saudi businessman, and has agreed to release $24 million in assets that the businessman, Mr. Saleh Idris, had deposited in U.S. banks.

On August 20 last year, the U.S. launched cruise missiles at Mr. Idris' pharmaceuticals plant in the Sudanese capital, Khartoum, and a camp in Afghanistan after bombs exploded at U.S. embassies in Nairobi, Kenya, and Dar es Salaam, Tanzania.

The U.S. alleged that both targets had links to the man they blamed for the Kenya and Tanzania bombs, Saudi millionaire Osama bin Laden, and that the Al Shifa plant in Khartoum manufactured chemical weapons.

The Al Shifa pharmaceuticals plant made both medicine and veterinary drugs, according to U.S. and European engineers and consultants who helped build, design and supply the plant.

The strikes came on the day that Monica Lewinsky gave evidence on her affair with President Bill Clinton, and bore a much noted resemblance to the movie *Wag the Dog*, in which a U.S. president diverts attention by starting a war.

Mr. Idris was represented by John Scanlon of the Washington law firm Akin Gump Strauss Hauer Feld, the same firm which employs Vernon Jordan, who gave evidence in defence of Mr Clinton in the Senate impeachment trial.

Mr. Idris had retained Kroll Associates, the world's leading firm of private investigators, to examine the evidence. Many of Kroll's employees are former intelligence and law enforcement officials of the British and American government, and it has also been hired by several governments, including the U.S. reports the *Independent*.

A legal case could have had major implications for Mr Clinton and for U.S. foreign policy. Facing a deadline to respond to the suit filed February 26, the Clinton administration chose not to contest it.

The Al Shifa plant had raised Sudan's self-sufficiency in medicine from 3 percent to over 50 percent and produced enough veterinary medicine for all of Africa.

Sudan has not been compensated for the deaths, lost jobs, and other financial losses resulting from lost production at the Al Shifa plant.

May 28, 1999

Milosevic Indicted, Clinton Poised to Sellout Kosovars

The indictment of Yugoslavia's President Milosevic by the United Nations war crimes tribunal is a victory for human rights, and for prosecutor Louise Arbour and her staff.

Milosevic and others are charged with the murder of over 340 Kosovar Muslims, aged between 2 and 95, and the deportation of 740,000 others in 1999 alone.

Also indicted are the president of Serbia, Milan Milutinovic; the deputy prime minister of Yugoslavia, Nikola Sainovic, a close aide of Milosevic; the chief of general staff of the Yugoslav army, Dragoljub Ojdanic; and Vlajko Stojiljkovic, the minister of internal affairs of Serbia.

But the indictment may do little to ease the plight of the Kosovar Muslims made homeless by Milosevic and his followers.

The UNHCR estimates that some 790,000 Muslims have left Kosovo since NATO began its air assault March 24. Many were displaced before the current exodus, and only about 10 per cent of Kosovo's 1.8 million Muslims remain in their homes in Kosovo.

In neighboring Bosnia and Herzegovina, another victim of Milosevic's rampaging Serbs, authorities expressed disappointment that the indictments did not cover acts committed there in the early 1990s.

The experience of the Bosnian Muslims may be an indicator of the West's commitment to easing the plight of the Kosovars.

In Bosnia, as in Kosovo, the West maintained an arms embargo on Milosevic and his Muslim victims. Thereby, the West prevented others from helping the Muslims being killed, raped, expelled from their homes, and stripped of identification papers and property records.

By the time the Dayton Peace Agreement was signed in December 1995, says the UNHCR, more than one million Bosnians had been displaced within the borders of Bosnia and Herzegovina, and at least one million more were living as refugees in some 25 other countries.

"An estimated 321,000 refugees and 253,000 internally displaced people returned to their homes in the three years following the signing of the Dayton Peace Agreement," says the UNHCR, "But there still remain around 400,000 refugees and over 840,000 displaced persons within Bosnia-Herzegovina, most of whom cannot go back to their home villages now controlled by the Serbs."

The Dayton Peace Agreement, forged after the killing of 200,000 Muslims, in effect, legitimized Serb aggression.

The agreement set aside the Bosnian constitution, and forced the multiparty, secular, parliamentary democracy of Bosnia to accept a secession of 49 percent of its territory to the Serbs. Today, as part of a 20,000 peacekeeping force, 6,000 U.S. troops are stationed in Bosnia, but they have yet to bring to trial indicted Serb warlords General Ratko Mladic and Radovan Karadjic who reside in a district controlled by NATO.

Now president Clinton, with his China and Russia policy in shambles, with NATO split on the use of ground forces in Kosovo, and with the U.S. Congress increasingly reluctant to back him, is desperate for a negotiated settlement.

Dealing with the KLA had limited NATO's options, as the KLA sought only independence for Kosovo. But with the release of Ibrahim Rugova, the "moderate" president of the self-styled Republic of Kosovo who had been under house arrest in Belgrade, the KLA have challenged the West's negotiations on their behalf.

President Clinton, having precipitated a humanitarian catastrophe, seems poised to declare victory with another Dayton type agreement, and sellout the Kosovars as he did the Bosnians. Prosecutor Louise Arbour has made a sellout more difficult for Mr. Clinton.

June 6, 1999

Winning and Losing in Yugoslavia

There was no doubt that if NATO chose to, it would prevail militarily, and it did, but it surrendered its primary objective—preventing a humanitarian catastrophe.

The NATO war machine, with funding of about $270 billion annually in the United States, and about $180 billion annually in the other NATO countries, prevailed militarily over Yugoslavia's armed forces which receive less than $1 billion annually.

Before the war began it was estimated that after 7 1/2 years of international economic sanctions, it would take Yugoslavia 29 years to reach the level of economic prosperity it had in 1989. Now the estimate is 45 years—without international aid, estimated at between $50 billion and $150 billion, to rebuild the war ravaged country.

Fought for a good cause—the prevention of a humanitarian catastrophe—NATO's air-only campaign hastened the process of ethnic cleansing begun by President Milosevic. U.S. generals had forewarned President Clinton that this would be the result.

Using the war as an excuse Yugoslav forces destroyed more than 500 villages, and raped, tortured, and killed thousands of Kosovar Muslims.

Perhaps 35,000 people had fled Kosovo in the months before the NATO bombing began. The UNHCR reported 4,000 registered refugees outside of Kosovo on March 27. Now only about 10 per cent of Kosovo's 1.8 million Muslims remain in their homes.

NATO forces, with the exception of the vaunted Apache helicopters, performed brilliantly. They killed 5000 Serbian soldiers, wounded 10,000, while the NATO count of deaths due to combat, not accident, was zero.

NATO's primary cause was just, but it was not a just war. NATO waged a war that had no reasonable chance of success in preventing a humanitarian catastrophe—its professed goal. NATO waged a war for reasons of self-interest—to perpetuate NATO which has no place in a post Cold War world.

NATO did not wage war as a last resort, having exhausted all non-violent means of settling the dispute with Yugoslavia. Under the G-8 plan for peace accepted by Yugoslavia, NATO accepted terms it refused to accept before the NATO ultimatum that triggered the war—no NATO access to all of Yugoslavia, and no vote for Kosovo's independence. As in Bosnia, arms to Kosovo's Muslims were embargoed.

NATO's peace plan is unacceptable to the KLA which served as NATO's allies on the ground. The Kosovars have no homes or businesses to return to, few crops and livestock to feed them, and are mentally scarred by what they have witnessed in the last several weeks.

Even if the G-8 plan holds the war is far from over. Will NATO countries, specifically their taxpayers, provide the funding to rebuild Yugoslavia? For how long will the Kosovars accept limited autonomy under NATO occupation? How long will an imposed "peace" last?

And what of President Milosevic and others indicted by the International Criminal Tribunal for the Former Yugoslavia? Will they be brought to trial? And what of the formal complaint laid before the Tribunal, by a group of lawyers from several countries, charging individual leaders of NATO countries and officials of NATO itself? Will it be properly processed?

What of the precedent set by NATO in intervening in the internal affairs of a sovereign Yugoslavia? Will this lead to more self-serving interference in the affairs of other states? Will it accelerate the arms race of which the U.S. is the primary beneficiary?

Winning and losing depends upon how one measures it.

The war in Yugoslavia was won like the attack on the Mount Carmel Center in Waco, Texas (April 19, 1993) was won. The cult leader and 80 followers, including women and children, died when their compound burned after U.S. government agents tried to flush them out with tear gas.

The war on Yugoslavia was a demonstration to the world of NATO, and more specifically U.S., credibility, and to justify increases in defense spending to which the U.S. Congress has readily acquiesced. There may have been genuine concern for Milosevic's ethnic cleansing, but NATO was unwilling to risk lives to prevent it.

Beginning with the Gulf War, 500 years after the fall of Muslim Spain in 1492, the Europeans and their descendants are on their second wave of expansion.

The first wave of European expansion, launched with professed good intentions, devastated the Americas, Asia, Africa, Australia, and China. The second wave, with the U.S. led NATO in the vanguard, is heading toward the natural resources of Russia and Central Asia—a somber prelude to the New Millennium.

["The Serbs would not accept a NATO force; NATO on its 50th anniversary wanted to show it mattered."—"Rambouillet Talks 'Designed to Fail'," *BBC News Online*, March 19, 2000]

August 28, 1999

U.S., Britain Widening War on Iraq

With only six months left before the start in earnest of the United States presidential election campaign, the U.S. and Britain are preparing for a large scale operation against Iraq, reports *Agence France-Presse*.

More than 500 U.S. air strikes this year alone, and $97 million to his opponents, have failed to topple Iraq's president Saddam Hussein. On August 19, U.S. warplanes, for the first time since December, struck positions outside the no-fly zones set up by the allied forces in northern and southern Iraq. International lawyers argue that these no-fly zones have not been sanctioned by the UN as claimed by the U.S.

Meanwhile, pressure has been growing to ease the sanctions on Iraq. A UNICEF survey released earlier this month found that "between 1984 and 1989, there were 56 deaths of children under 5 per 1,000 live births compared to 131 deaths per 1,000 live births from 1994 to 1999." More than 1.5 million are reported to have died as a result of U.S. forced UN sanctions on Iraq.

The *Associated Press* reports that the head of the UN's humanitarian program, France, and other members of the Security Council have expressed desperation with the United States for placing on hold hundreds of aid contracts worth millions of dollars.

Former U.S. Attorney General Ramsey Clark in his August 29 letter to the UN Security Council says, "The UN is inviting a world ordered by the diplomacy of cruise missiles and economic strangulation, governance by deadly high tech military assaults which are indefensible, and foreign imposed hunger and pestilence. The Superpower scofflaw responsible for both crimes is the same deadbeat that refuses to pay its UN dues, directs the creation of ad hoc UN criminal tribunals not authorized by UN Charter to pursue its chosen enemies and refuses to participate in an International Criminal Tribunal created by treaty approved by 120 nations for fear that it might be held accountable under the rule of law."

At a mid-September meeting of the UN Security Council, Britain is expected to submit a US-backed resolution on Iraq which will provide the U.S. and Britain with a new legal tool to take measures against Iraq, reports *AFP*.

The British proposal calls for the creation of a so-called "United Nations Commission on Inspection and Monitoring" (UNCIM) to replace the current weapons inspection committee. Iraq calls the proposal "monstrous" charging that it is aimed at increasing restrictions on the country.

Meanwhile, despite objections from the U.S. Department of State, five staff members of the U.S. House of Representatives, accompanied by Kathy Kelly of Voices In the Wilderness, and Phyllis Bennis of the

Washington-based Institute for Policy Studies, are on their way to Iraq to assess the situation first hand. The staff members work for Reps. Sam Gejdenson, D-Conn.; Cynthia McKinney, D-Ga.; Earl Hilliard, D-Ala.; Danny K. Davis, D-Ill.; and Bernard Sanders, I-Vt.

The U.S. is also urging the Pope to drop his plans to visit the ancient Iraqi town of Ur, where the Bible says Abraham was born, as part of the new millennium celebrations.

September 9, 1999

FBI May Eliminate Dagestani Websites

The U.S. Federal Bureau of Investigation, reports *BBC News Online*, has offered to help Russia "in eliminating Websites set up by Islamic militants fighting in the southern republic of Dagestan."

The "Muslim peoples of the Caucasus—Chechen, Ingush, Circassians, Abkhaz, Dagestanis—have been in almost constant revolt against their Russian colonial rulers for three centuries," writes Eric Margolis of the *Toronto Sun*.

"Russia crushed all revolts with ruthless ferocity and twice attempted genocide," says Mr. Margolis, and in "the 1940s, Stalin deported nearly all the 1.5-million Chechen to Siberian concentration camps, where 25 percent died. Two million other Soviet Muslims, including many Dagestanis, were also sent in cattle cars to Stalin's death camps. Hitler used gas; Stalin used the Russian winter."

Now it appears that the FBI may deny Dagestani freedom fighters their right to free speech, and deny interested readers access to information from all relevant sources.

During NATO's recent war with Yugoslavia the information coming out of Belgrade, Yugoslavia's capital, was more accurate than that coming from NATO.

"Belgrade's claims of 76 losses represent only about a fivefold exaggeration," says Alan J. Kuperman, Research Fellow at the Brookings Institution, while "NATO's original claims represent up to a twentyfold exaggeration."

September 11, 1999

Foreign Interests Could Lead to Indonesia's Breakup

Foreign interests could lead to a breakup of Indonesia, and precipitate a much wider catastrophe than is now occurring in East Timor.

According to Oxford Analytica, a British political consulting firm, Indonesia blames Australia for "putting pressure on [Indonesia's President] Habibie through a letter sent by Prime Minister John Howard urging that a referendum be held in the territory [East Timor]."

Indonesia fears that Australia may be seeking the means to weaken it. Australia has the motive, Indonesians believe, and in the turmoil in East Timor Australia sees opportunity. But without U.S./UN backing it lacks the means.

Indonesian President "Habibie and his civilian advisors, many of them drawn from the Association of Indonesian Muslim Intellectuals, have long argued that Catholic East Timor should be allowed to go its own way," says Oxford Analytica. Others fear that independence for East Timor "will set a disturbing precedent for other restive regions such as Irian Jaya and Aceh."

Aceh has been racked with violence. The Achenese seek a greater share of profits from Aceh's oil, and some seek outright independence from Indonesia.

Australia's offer to lead a UN peacekeeping force to East Timor is viewed with suspicion. About 200 years ago, aboriginals occupied all of Australia and the island of Tasmania. In Tasmania, following the arrival of the British—ancestors of today's white Australians, not a single Aborigine survived, while those located on the coasts of mainland Australia were forced to flee inland or were killed.

Indonesia, with a population of 213 million, and 17,000 islands (6,000 inhabited) stretching for about 5,000 kilometers, "fears that Canberra is seeking to ally itself with East Timor so that it can take the best advantage of any future breakup of Indonesia."

The U.S. has its own interests in Indonesia, and shares responsibility for the events leading to the present situation in East Timor.

"American strategy in Asia," argues Stratfor.com—an intelligence consulting firm based in Austin, Texas—"is focused on control of the archipelago of islands that runs down East Asia's coast. Starting with the Aleutians, the line runs through Japan, Taiwan, the Philippines, Indonesia, and is ultimately anchored on Singapore. Control of this line allows the U.S. to achieve three things."

"First, it provides the U.S. with a comprehensive line beyond which Chinese and Russian naval power cannot move in time of war. Second, the line provides the U.S. with offensive positions from which to threaten air and naval actions against the continent and even, should the need arise, occasional amphibious interventions along East Asia's coast. Finally, and perhaps most importantly, it gives the U.S. implicit power over petroleum-hungry East Asia by placing the essential maritime choke points in the hands of U.S. naval forces."

The Asian financial crisis in 1997/98 revealed the weak underpinnings of Indonesia's economy, a large part of which is in the hands of ethnic Chinese, and not the native majority Muslims. Indonesia brokered a $42 billion bailout package from the International Monetary Fund. Now this loan package has been jeopardized, and continued weakness in Indonesia's economy may trigger widespread unrest.

Meanwhile, President B. J. Habibie appears not to have full control, while Indonesia's military which plays a powerful role is adjusting to changes brought about when President Habbibie took over from President Suharto. Now Ms. Sukarnoputri, daughter of Indonesia's first President Sukarno, hopes to take over from President Habibie following a vote by the People's Consultative Assembly in November.

"The Indonesian fascist army is a monster that was created by Washington in the 1960s, when the U.S. was escalating the war in Vietnam," says former U.S. Attorney General Ramsey Clark. He adds, "Washington tipped the balance toward the fascist right wing of the military by training, equipping and financing a coup," which replaced President Sukarno with the U.S. favored President Suharto.

Suharto's army invaded East Timor in 1975 following its decolonization from Portugal (which obtained East Timor in an 1859 treaty with the Netherlands), and the outbreak of civil war between pro- and anti-Marxist groups. The U.S., which viewed East Timor as another Cuba, looked the other way.

The Indonesia which emerged from years of Dutch colonial oppression in 1949 is a mix of cultures as diverse as those of say Washington, DC and the Indians of the Amazon forest. It is now in the midst of a volatile situation that could worsen, and destroy the fragile ties which bind Indonesia.

Provided that there have been no irregularities, Indonesia has little choice but to abide by its agreement with Portugal and the UN regarding the future of East Timor. But attempts to breakup Indonesia are likely to precipitate a much wider catastrophe than is now occurring in East Timor.

The first priority for Indonesia, and the international community, is to minimize harm to the people of East Timor and all of Indonesia. And it's in Indonesia's self interest to set aside internal divisions, and to be at the forefront of the solution to the problems in East Timor, Aceh, and Irian Jaya.

September 15, 1999

One Million Indonesians Died in U.S. Backed Coup

One million Indonesians are reported to have died in the U.S. backed coup that led to the Suharto presidency, and the occupation of East Timor.

Aid agencies estimate (*BBC News Online*, September 13) that between 600 and 7,000 people have been killed and as many as 300,000 have fled their homes since the UN-backed August 30 referendum on East Timor's future.

Now pro-Jakarta militias, angered by President Habibie's decision to allow international peacekeepers into East Timor, have told aid workers (*The Times*, September 14) that they will take revenge by embarking on a violent killing spree in West Timor. Should this occur, would the UN-approved, Australia-led, multinational force extend operations to West Timor?

The wider catastrophe we fear may become reality, and the likely winners will not be the Indonesians who suffered under 350 years of colonial oppression, and had their lives shattered once again when U.S.-backed Suharto assumed the presidency and ousted President Sukarno.

G. C. Allan and Audrey Donnithorne, in *Western Enterprise in Indonesia and Malaya*, write "In 1940 only 240 Indonesian students graduated from the high schools and only 37 from the colleges. In that year, out of over 3,000 higher civil servants there were only 221 Indonesians, and even in the middle ranks a larger number of posts were held by Europeans and Eurasians, who counted as Dutch."

By 1945, writes Reba Lewis, author of *Indonesia: Troubled Paradise*, 93 percent of the people were still illiterate. After 350 years of colonial domination, there were only a hundred Indonesian physicians; less than a hundred Indonesian engineers; and, in a nation dependent upon the efficiency of its land productivity, only ten Indonesian agricultural experts.

Indonesia proclaimed independence on August 17, 1945, and on December 27, 1949, Indonesia became legally independent from the Netherlands (Holland).

In 1958, the U.S. attempted to oust Sukarno. Thomas Ross and David Wise in their book *The Invisible Government*, relate how in 1958 the U.S. supplied a right-wing rebel force in Indonesia with arms and a small air force of B-26 bombers for the failed attempt.

Deirdre Griswold says, in *The Second Greatest Crime of the Century*, "Between October 1, 1965, and April or May of the following year, the right-wing military regime of Generals Nasution and Suharto seized power and consolidated its strength in Indonesia. In that scant seven months as many as a million people were slaughtered. The rising toll of victims appeared occasionally in the press here, recorded with little more passion than a sports score."

Until the 1965 coup, Indonesia was one of the most dynamic countries. "The Sukarno government," writes Ms. Griswold, "took a number of bold steps in foreign policy that shocked the Western capitals and threatened to be infectious. Indonesia withdrew from both the UN and the Olympic games, declaring them to be dominated by imperialism, and started to set up rival international bodies. At the very moment that the right-wing coup was taking place, a conference against foreign military bases, which of course was aimed first and foremost at the U.S. with its 3,000 [?] installations overseas, was in session in Djakarta."

After twenty-five years of fighting the Japanese, the Dutch and the U.S. imperialists, the 1965 coup and the subsequent slaughter of a million Indonesians, paved the way for U.S. companies who, in 1966, began arriving for "the feast," writes Ms. Griswold.

Unilever setup oil and edible fat plants. Uniroyal got its rubber plantation and latex plant. Union Carbide, Singer Sewing Machine and National Cash Register got back properties expropriated during the revolution. Eastern Airlines partnered with the Indonesia airline Garuda; Mobil Oil secured oil exploration rights. For a mere $75 million, Freeport Sulphur got a contract for exploiting West Irian copper which is 20 times as rich as ores found in Arizona and Utah. Freeport claims it has since paid nearly $1.7 billion in direct benefits (taxes, dividends, royalties) to the Government of Indonesia.

The U.S. armed, trained Suharto military invaded the former Portuguese colony of East Timor in 1975 to stop a civil war between pro- and anti-Marxist groups. President Suharto did what his Western mentors had done to acquire colonies or to consolidate their own state boundaries, and 200,000 East Timorese are reported to have been killed resisting the Indonesian occupation.

Wrongs cannot be righted until the facts are known and understood. Peace and social justice cannot prevail until the rich and powerful set an example for the weak and impoverished.

September 22, 1999

Greed at Core of Indonesia's Timor Problem

At its core the problem of East Timor, and indeed much of Indonesia, has a lot to do with greed rather than the Muslim-Christian divide portrayed in the media.

From the first century AD, until the 16th, Indonesia was comprised of various Hindu kingdoms. The Hindu-Buddhist kingdom of Sriwijaya, on Sumatra, rose in the 7th century AD. The Hindu Mataram dynasty flourished in the plains of Central Java between the 8th and 10th centuries AD. Founded in the late 13th century, the Majapahit Empire, the last of the Hindu kingdoms, became the most powerful.

Sumatra was then known as the "Island of Gold," and Java as the "Rice Island."

Muslim traders began arriving in the 13th century, and Islam spread peacefully through the islands. Descendants of some Hindu kingdoms retreated to the islands of Bali and Lombok where they flourish to this day. In the early 16th century the Hindu kingdom of Mataram converted to Islam.

With the fall of Muslim Spain in 1492 (as in the Americas, Africa, and South Asia), came 350 years of brutal colonial rule and exploitation. First to arrive were the Portuguese in 1511 AD. The Portuguese were followed by the Dutch (1602 to 1799 AD), the British (1811 to 1815 AD), and again the Dutch (1816 to 1908 AD).

The colonial masters took slaves, forced the natives to grow crops for export which resulted in famines, and destroyed the thriving inter-island trade.

By 1908 nationalist movements began seeking self-government, and Indonesia declared independence on August 17, 1947. Sukarno, a leader of the independence movement, became president. He was overthrown in 1965 by Suharto in a U.S.-backed military coup in which it is reported that one million people, mainly Chinese, were killed.

When the Dutch and Portuguese formally partitioned East Timor between them in the 19th century, East Timor remained a part of the Portuguese colony. The governor of Portuguese Timor, in 1974, granted permission for political parties, and five emerged.

Said to be lacking popular support, the Fretilin party, seeking independence from Indonesia, resorted to terror. Civil war broke out, and on August 27, 1975, the governor and Portuguese officials abandoned the capital Dili. The U.S. armed, trained Indonesian military intervened. It is reported that between 70,000 and 200,000 Timorese were killed in subsequent fighting.

Fretilin, supplied with arms from the Portuguese army arsenal, declared East Timor independent. The four other parties in East Timor declared their independence and integration with Indonesia. East Timor became the 27th province of Indonesia, but this claim was not recognized by the UN.

Rich in natural resources, Indonesia's primary problem is the equitable sharing of these resources. Foreign interests, and internal corruption, add to the inherent difficulty that while Java is Indonesia's most heavily populated island, many of the resources are located in less populated islands.

According to former U.S. Ambassador to Indonesia, Edward Masters, Indonesia did more in 35 years to develop barren, infertile East Timor than Portugal did in four centuries.

Indonesia allocated development funds to East Timor at a rate six times the national average. In 1975, less than 10% of Timorese were literate, there were only 50 schools, and no colleges. By 1994 East Timor had 600 elementary schools, 90 middle schools and three colleges. Under the Portuguese East, Timor had only two hospitals and 14 health clinics. By 1994, there were 10 hospitals and nearly 200 village health centers. In 1975, it had 20 km hard surfaced roads, by 1994 there were 500 km. The number of Catholic Churches in predominantly Catholic East Timor quadrupled under Indonesian rule

But the Fretilin party continued to resist Indonesian rule, and offshore oil discoveries attracted foreign interests.

"Australian oil technicians say that the Timor seabed could yield some of the world's most productive oil fields," reported the Multinational Monitor. A treaty was signed in 1989 by Australia and Indonesia. This Timor Gap Treaty came into force in 1991 and is due for review in 2031. Australia needs this oil, and massive revenues are said to flow to both governments. Independence for East Timor would likely give it a larger share of these revenues.

The division of natural resources is also at the core of secessionist movements in Aceh, Irian Jaya, and in the neighboring Philippines.

On Aceh in 1971, Mobil Oil discovered one of the world's richest onshore reserves of natural gas, estimated at 40 billion cubic meters. Aceh provides an estimated 11% of Indonesia's total exports, but less than 10% of this wealth is reinvested in the province. Mobil Oil is reported to have caused massive environmental damage, and is said to be linked to the Indonesian military's land seizures, bombings, and massacres.

On Irian Jaya, military repression, and massive environmental damage has been linked to Freeport McMoRan, a Louisiana corporation.

In April 1967, Freeport McMoRan became the first foreign company granted an operating permit following the 1965–1966 U.S.-backed coup that installed General Suharto. Former U.S. Secretary of State Henry Kissinger is credited with having introduced company officials to President Suharto. According to Paul S. Murphy, Senior Vice President, Mr. Kissinger sits on Freeport's board earning $25,000 a year, and is paid an annual retainer of $200,000 for consultation work.

In 1999, Freeport McMoRan received approval to almost double production, which will increase land seizures and environmental damage. With reserves valued at $40 billion, the Freeport project is the largest single gold deposit in the world and the third largest open-cut copper mine.

In the neighboring Philippines, National Steel Company, writes Fred Hill author of *Teasing the Tiger: A Third World Study of Muslim Mindanao*, the Philippines' largest steel mill is destroying Lake Lanao—essential for the survival of neighboring communities. Located in the Muslim countryside, it is the major employer in the area. But except for 5 or 10 Muslims its 4,000 employees are Christian Visayans, many of whom were brought there in the 1970s. The media publish reports about Muslim violence in Mindanao, but not the reasons for their frustration.

And similarly in East Timor the violence has little if anything to do with Muslim-Christian enmity. Christians live in peace with Muslims in West Timor, and elsewhere in Indonesia. About half of the pro-Indonesian militia leaders have Christian names. Greed, the greed of corporations, government officials, individuals is at the core of problems. The religion card is used to divide, rule, and exploit the people and the land—just like colonial rulers did in earlier times.

[Prime Minister John Howard's announcement that "Australia will act as the United States' 'deputy sheriff' in regional peacekeeping" has Indonesians convinced that Canberra wants to take over East Timor to establish a colonial foothold....David McGibbon, chairman of Australia's Joint Parliamentary Foreign Affairs Committee, said: 'The real danger we face in all this is being seen as a post-colonial relic, isolated from Asia in a corner of the Pacific.'"—David Watt, Howard's 'Sheriff' Role Angers Asians," *Times*, September 27, 1999]

["Australia estimates the death toll in the violent aftermath of East Timor's August 30 self-rule ballot at between 500 and 1,000, Foreign Minister Alexander Downer said Wednesday. Downer rejected claims that Indonesian forces and their militia allies massacred tens of thousands of people and had dumped thousands of bodies at sea, saying they would inevitably have washed ashore eventually."—"Australia Estimates East Timor Death Toll at 500 to 1,000," *AFP*, December 1, 1999]

September 28, 1999

America's Disgraceful Silence over Chechnya

America's silence over Russia's indiscriminate bombing of Chechnya, even as "peacekeepers" undertake their "humanitarian intervention" in East Timor, is a disgrace.

"Russian jets pounded dozens of Chechen targets yesterday," reports the *Times* of London, as a swelling flood of refugees headed for a border that Russia is fortifying as if for war. Two big oil refineries, three bridges and a half-built television centre in Grozny were destroyed in the fifth consecutive day of bombing." Experts say that Moscow may be hoping to fight a sophisticated air war modeled on NATO's Kosovo campaign.

BBC News Online is reporting a "humanitarian catastrophe in Chechnya" where 30,000 to 100,000 Chechens have fled into the neighboring southern Russian republic of Ingushetia.

Following a recent spate of bombings in Russian cities, which killed 300 people, Russian police have arrested more than 100 people, while thousands who look like Chechens have been interrogated. Chechen officials deny that they are behind the killings.

The Chechens, a distinct ethnic group who have lived in the mountains and plains of Chechnya since the first millennium B.C., have endured 250 years of savage Russian colonial rule writes Peter Daniel DiPaola, in *A Noble Sacrifice? Jus ad Bellum and the International Community's Gamble in Chechnya*. The Chechens are a subjugated people. They have fought continual wars of independence against the Russians.

In 1944, Stalin deported the Chechens and Ingush to Central Asia and dissolved the Chechen-Ingush republic. About 25 percent of the deported Chechens and Ingush died in exile or enroute. They have also been the victims of widespread job and educational discrimination.

In their 1994–1996 war for independence, says Aleksander I. Lebed, the former Russian security chief, "about 80,000 people had been killed in the fighting and that some 240,000 had been wounded."

President Clinton supported Russia's 1994–1996 war in Chechnya. He personally pushed a new, $10.2 billion loan for Yeltsin through the International Monetary Fund saying that he backed Russia's need to "maintain its territorial integrity." He had no such qualms regarding Indonesia's integrity when he threatened to delay a $42 billion IMF loan package to get Indonesia to agree to the Australia-led UN occupation of East Timor.

Neither the Chechen freedom fighters, nor their support of neighboring Dagestan's quest for independence from Russia gets any encouragement from the West. There is no talk of withholding IMF loans. The U.S. has offered Russia "technical and investigative assistance" in its investigation of the explosions reports the *Associated Press*. But the U.S. offer of help in shutting down Dagestani web sites is hardly in keeping with America's professed ideal of free speech.

According to David Hoffman of the *Washington Post*, political commentator Andrei Piontkovsky says that Russia will bomb "Chechnya into the Stone Age. Unfortunately, I am sure this is the thing they are certain to do now. The Chechens will react with more bombs. Moscow will react with pogroms against people from the Caucasus."

Reports Eric Margolis of the *Toronto Sun*, the respected Georgian writer, Melor Sturua, a columnist for the leading Russian newspaper *Izvestia*, wrote of America's disgraceful silence over Chechnya: "I remember a time when the arrest of even one Soviet dissident would create a storm of indignation here (in the US). Soviet embassies were picketed, Soviet goods boycotted, Soviet crimes were condemned." Congress imposed trade sanctions on the USSR to force it to allow Jewish emigration to Israel.

Unfortunately the Chechens do not have anything like the Israeli lobby to advance their cause, and Chechnya just happens to be a gateway to the Caspian Sea oil worth between $2 trillion and $4 trillion at 1997 market prices.

["Geologists are not sure exactly how much oil is available for extraction in the Caspian Sea region--some say 40 billion barrels (about twice the amount found in the North Sea area), some say 100 billion and some claim that as much as 200 billion barrels are waiting to be tapped there."—Michael T. Klare, author of *Resource Wars: Global Geopolitics in the 21st Century*]

["Russia's state-owned Rosneft oil company announced yesterday that it has been given the right to exploit and export Chechnya's substantial oil and gas reserves."— Giles Whittell, "Fleeing Chechens 'caught in snowy death trap'," *The Times*, February 9, 2000]

November 14, 1999

U.S. Supporting Russia's Genocidal War in Chechnya

The United States, by its attacks on Afghanistan, Sudan, and Yugoslavia, and by its continuing war on Iraq, set the example, is providing billions in aid to Russia, and must share responsibility for Russia's genocidal war on Chechnya.

On September 18, following a meeting between Russian investigators and officials at the FBI, the *Associated Press* reported that the State Department and FBI chief Louis Freeh offered "technical and investigative assistance" to the Russian government in its investigation of four explosions in apartment buildings in Moscow that killed more than 300 people.

Russian authorities accuse Chechen freedom fighters of being responsible for the bombings. The Chechens have denied responsibility, but are, according to analysts at Stratfor.com, "the preferred scapegoat."

A state of emergency could benefit president Yeltsin, who would like to see the December elections postponed until he can ensure a loyal successor.

According to Stratfor.com "Yeltsin's opponents, such as former Prime Minister Yevgeny Primakov, have long feared that Yeltsin would call a state of emergency for political gain. The recent bombings could give him the excuse to do this legitimately."

Despite the lack of evidence against the Chechens, and the May 1997 treaty granting Chechnya de facto independence, Russia launched massive, indiscriminate attacks on Chechnya.

BBC News Online reports that refugees arriving at the border with the neighboring republic of Ingushetia have been giving "consistent accounts of death and destruction caused by Russian troops." Refugees say people are being killed as they try to flee the Russian bombardment.

An estimated 200,000 refugees have fled to Ingushetia. About 3,000 have been killed, and 10,000 wounded. Chechnya's president, Aslan Maskhadov, has appealed to President Clinton to halt the "genocide of the Chechen people."

The Russian prime minister, Vladimir Putin, cites the U.S. example to justify the attack on Chechnya. Says Mr. Putin, "Exactly the same tactics were deployed during Operation Desert Storm, in the bombing of the former Yugoslavia, and in the various United States attempts to strike back at the world's most wanted terrorist—Osama bin Laden."

Meanwhile billions in U.S. dollars continue to flow to Russia through the International Monetary Fund.

Contrast this with President Clinton's threat to delay a $42 billion IMF loan package to get Indonesia to agree to the UN intervention in East Timor. And now reports have emerged that the recent killings in East Timor were greatly exaggerated—presumably to justify UN intervention.

Contrast this also with the UN sanctions initiated today against Afghanistan for its refusal to surrender Osama bin Laden to the U.S. The U.S. accuses bin Laden of masterminding the bombing of U.S. embassies in Kenya and Tanzania, but refuses to provide evidence to back its claim.

"The Chechen people are now standing on the threshold of total destruction," says foreign minister Iyas Akhmadov.

["Authorities estimate that only a few thousand of the more than 500,000 people who lived here in early fall are left."—Sharon LaFraniere, "Little Life Left Amid Grozny's Hollow Ruins," *Washington Post*, March 1, 2000]

["The president has not undertaken a single concrete action to demonstrate U.S. opposition to Russia's cruel war."—William V. Roth Jr., "Actions, Not Words," *Washington Post*, March 18, 2000]

November 16, 1999

EgyptAir 990 Pilot's Prayer Indicates Criminal Act?

A Muslim pilot's prayer as an EgyptAir plane was going down is said to point toward a criminal act, and the investigation into last month's crash off Massachusetts may be turned over to the U.S. Federal Bureau of Investigations.

Today's *Washington Post* carries a front page, above the fold headline: "Pilot Prayed, Then Shut Off Jets Autopilot." The article states that "voice and data recorders from EgyptAir Flight 990 reveal that just before one of the pilots, apparently alone in the cockpit, turned off the autopilot, he uttered a very short Muslim prayer, government sources said. National Transportation Safety Board officials found the evidence so disturbing they are considering turning the probe over to the FBI."

ABC's Washington affiliate displayed the words of the Islamic prayer, known as the *shahadah*, as the prayer uttered by the EgyptAir pilot. *Agence France-Presse* quoted an airline official saying the prayer was the *shahadah*.

Aviation experts have stated that there could be several reasons for taking the plane off autopilot, and shutting down the engines, but the utterance of the *shahadah* has caused the NTSB/FBI team to classify the investigation as a criminal matter.

If this is all the evidence available to date, then this is a grievous act of bigotry by top officials of the U.S. government. Had they reached similar conclusions based upon a Jewish or Christian pilot's prayer, U.S. congressmen and media would be demanding that these officials be terminated.

A Hindu, Buddhist, Jew, or Christian may well utter a prayer when confronted with a potentially deadly situation. A prayer so uttered is not in itself evidence of a deliberate criminal act.

What may be criminal is to rule out other explanations for the crash. At this stage all options should be kept open, but speculation on the basis of a prayer uttered by the pilot is at the very least irresponsible.

The *shahadah* is one of the five "pillars of Islam." It is a short prayer: "There is no god but God; Muhammad is the Messenger of God." The four other pillars of Islam are prayer five times daily, fasting, alms-giving, and the pilgrimage to Mecca.

To become a Muslim, one has only to recite the *shahadah*. Like the pilgrimage to Mecca, it is required only once in a lifetime. However, pious Muslims recite the *shahadah* throughout their lives, even as often as several times each day—particularly in times of distress. Sufis, Islam's mystics, use the first part of the *shahadah*, "There is no god but God," repeatedly in their chanting. The *shahadah* is recited as one is dying, and if one cannot do so someone else may recite the *shahadah* for them.

It is normal for the Muslim pilot of EgyptAir 990 to have uttered the *shahadah* if confronted with a deadly situation beyond his control. What is not normal is to consider this prayer as an indication of a criminal act.

Normally, the transfer of an investigation from one agency to another would not be a matter of concern. But we question the transfer of the investigation to the FBI, whose case against the blind Egyptian, Muslim cleric Sheikh Rahman was not one which would inspire confidence.

The *New York Times* reported that there was scant evidence that Sheikh Rahman even knew of the plan to bomb the World Trade Center, and other buildings in New York. The government's primary witness against Sheikh Rahman was an FBI informant, Mr. Emad Salem, who confessed to lying under oath in a previous trial. Six months before the World Trade Center bombing, the FBI terminated Mr. Salem after he failed several lie detector tests. Following the bombing, Mr. Salem was rehired for a fee of over $1 million.

The *shahadah* is the last sentence of The Wisdom Fund's 600 word introduction to Islam, known as "The Truth About Islam." It is available on the Internet at www.twf.org, and has been displayed in international journals and in Washington Metro rail stations.

November 26, 1999

Alternative Theories Emerge for EgyptAir 990 Crash

After 10 days of Muslim bashing—following the *Washington Post's* November 16 front page, above the fold headline which read: "Pilot Prayed, Then Shut Off Jets Autopilot"—alternative theories have begun to emerge for the October 31 crash of EgyptAir 990.

That evening, following the *Washington Post's* lead, relief pilot Gameel el-Batouty's prayer, identified as the *shahadah* (There is no god but God. Muhammad is the Messenger of God.) appeared on television screens with the clear implication that the utterance of this short prayer indicated a deliberate act of suicide and murder.

But the very next day, November 17, ABC's Washington affiliate stated that the pilot had said, "I have made my decision. Now I put my faith in God's hands." It is not clear whether the pilot also uttered the shahadah, or whether his utterance was incorrectly reported yesterday.

The National Transportation Safety Board advisory released November 17 indicated that the cockpit voice recorder (CVR) working group expected to have a transcript completed next week.

The flight data recorder (FDR) showed that the Boeing 767-300 pitch attitude moved from 40 degrees nose down to 10 degrees nose down. The speed brake handle moved from the stowed position to the deployed position. The last altitude registered was about 16,400 feet, at which time the aircraft was traveling at 574 knots.

The elevator split, which had previously been reported, was further defined by the FDR group. During the last 15 seconds, maximum split between the elevators was about 7 degrees and appeared to be lessening.

While the aircraft was at 33,000 feet, the autopilot cut off. Eight seconds later, the elevator moved into the nose down position, and the throttle was pulled back. Fourteen seconds after the nose down movement began, the aircraft reached Mach 0.86 and the master warning sounded. Thirteen seconds later, the engine start lever went to the "off" position. Fourteen seconds after that, the FDR, CVR and transponder shut off. From autopilot cutoff to end of data was about 50 seconds.

However, the lack of necessary facts did not deter U.S. media speculation.

The media consensus seemed to be that the pilot was depressed because he had been passed over for promotion, he had financial problems because of his child's health condition, and this drove him to crash the plane into the Atlantic.

These theories were challenged by his family who claimed that the pilot was financially well off, and they took television crews on a tour of the home Mr. Batouty had built for his upcoming retirement.

Still for the past ten days the recitation of an Islamic prayer, repeatedly mentioned by the media, confirmed for them the pilot's state of mind. *Newsweek* magazine based its cover story on the assertion that the pilot recited "Tawakilt ala allah" (I put my trust in God) 14 times.

Now doubts about who said what, and other theories have begun to emerge.

The London based *Independent* reported on November 20 (Andrew Marshall, "Doubt Cast on Suicide Theory for Air Crash"): "The American theory turns on a few facts whose interpretation is disputed. The cockpit voice recorders apparently show that the aircraft's captain, Ahmed al-Habashi, left the flight deck, leaving the relief copilot, Gamil al-Batouti, at the controls. He had been reported to have said "I made my decision now", before repeating a Muslim prayer variously translated as 'I put my faith in God's hands' or 'I depend on God'."

"But yesterday," said the *Independent*, "an unnamed official told news agencies that Mr. Batouti did not say 'I made my decision now' casting some doubt on the pilot suicide theory."

The *Star-Ledger* of Newark, NJ (Michael Hedges, "Pilot Who Saved Jet in '79 Says: Be Wary Of Crash Probe Theories," November 23) described an event where a "Boeing jetliner had leveled off above 30,000 feet after leaving New York when, mysteriously, it began a steep and terrifying descent, falling at speeds that briefly topped 800 mph."

The *Star-Ledger* goes on to say, "The aftermath of that incident two decades ago has caused [the pilot Harvey 'Hoot'] Gibson to be skeptical of quick explanations for aircraft crashes, like the theory that EgyptAir Flight 990 was downed October 31 by a suicidal pilot....Gibson says he believes his flight suffered from some sort of rudder failure, the cause in later years of at least two airline crashes involving Boeing 737s....It was the same rudder on the 727 as the 737."

On November 24, the *Associated Press* reported ("Egyptian Expert Offers Blast Theory") that "Gen. Issam Ahmed, head of the country's flight training program, urged Egyptian investigators to look closely at what happened in the rear of the plane and not to let their U.S. counterparts impose the suicide scenario." Said the general, "The two pilots took the right steps, including turning off the autopilot and the engines in an attempt to control the plane."

Today, November 26, Mr. Gibson and Gen. Issam Ahmed have been joined by others challenging reckless media speculation.

The *Washington Times* reported today on its front page ("Austrians Offer Malfunction Theory of EgyptAir Crash") that the "crash of EgyptAir Flight 990 might have been caused by a flight stabilizer breakdown that could have sent the plane plunging into the sea, an Austrian institute said yesterday."

The independent Austrian Institute of Aerospace Medicine and Space Biology said, "The abnormal dive of the Boeing 767 could be due to a so-called 'stabilizer runaway....The stabilizer runaway batters the plane so strongly that the autopilot is insufficiently strong and it is automatically turned off on purpose in such a case."

FOX News reported ("Airline Pilots' Group Hits Out at EgyptAir Probe") that an "international airline pilots' group Friday stepped into the controversy over the probe into the EgyptAir flight 990 crash, denouncing what it said was a media frenzy about suicide as a cause."

Captain Ted Murphy of the International Federation of Airline Pilots' Associations told *Reuters*, "The big issue is the failure of the industry to resist the temptation to talk. Authorities have to resist giving an answer straight away."

Faced with these emerging theories the *Washington Post* began backing off from its earlier focus on the pilot's prayer. The Post (David A. Vise and Don Phillips, "No Letup For FBI In Probe Of Crash") said: "While his prayer in Arabic—I have put my faith in God's hands—has played a role in the probe, it is less significant, officials said, than the actions he took in the cockpit."

As we said on November 16, "What may be criminal is to rule out other explanations for the crash. At this stage all options should be kept open, but speculation on the basis of a prayer uttered by the pilot is at the very least irresponsible."

November 30, 1999

EgyptAir 990: FAA Order Raises New Questions

The Federal Aviation Administration yesterday ordered a special inspection of Boeing Co. after a series of quality-control problems, including the discovery by American Airlines mechanics of 16 improperly tightened bolts in a Boeing 767 tail section, reports Don Phillips ("FAA Calls a Special Inspection of Boeing," *Washington Post*, November 30).

Boeing has determined that an incorrect torque wrench had been used because of a difference between Boeing requirements and the work instructions given to workers.

The FAA ordered inspection gives some credence to questions raised about the stabilizer of the Boeing 767 involved in the EgyptAir 990 crash.

Less than a week ago the independent Austrian Institute of Aerospace Medicine and Space Biology said that "the abnormal dive of the Boeing 767 could be due to a so-called 'stabilizer runaway.'...The stabilizer runaway batters the plane so strongly that the autopilot is insufficiently strong and it is automatically turned off on purpose in such a case."

And an international airline pilots group has stepped into the controversy over the probe into the EgyptAir flight 990 crash, denouncing what it said was a media frenzy about suicide as a cause."

Captain Ted Murphy of the International Federation of Airline Pilots' Associations told *Reuters*, "The big issue is the failure of the industry to resist the temptation to talk. Authorities have to resist giving an answer straight away."

This is not the first time that U.S. government officials and media have jumped to hasty conclusions.

Five months after the December 21, 1988, explosion of Pan Am Flight 103 over Lockerbie, Scotland, the U.S. State Department announced that the CIA was confident that the villains were members of the Popular Front for the Liberation of Palestine led by Ahmed Jibril based in Syria. But when Syria allied with the U.S. in the Gulf War the blame was shifted to Libya.

When TWA 800 crashed in 1996, the *Washington Post*, in it's July 23 editorial, stated that while the "evidence of terrorism is not yet there," that "courtroom-type proof" may be hard to come by, that "international validation before the act of punishment would be the best way to go, but if that is not feasible a national decision by the injured party, the United States, ought to suffice."

There is one thing of which we may be reasonably sure. The cause of such crashes may never be determined with certainty.

Newsweek magazine, in their cover story of November 29 by Daniel Klaidman and Mark Hosenball, "I Put My Trust in God," on the crash of EgyptAir 990, state, "Nearly three years after the NTSB determined that a faulty fuel tank aboard the Boeing 747 caused the explosion that destroyed TWA Flight 800 in July 1996, Boeing is still trying to prove that the plane was brought down by a missile or a bomb."

Boeing's concerns are echoed by the Associated Retired Aviation Professionals which states: "Recently uncovered information now shows that TWA Flight 800 could have been shot down by one or more shoulder-fired missiles." The association's membership includes Admiral Thomas Moorer former Chairman of the U.S. Joint Chief's of Staff.

According to *Time* magazine (Johanna McGeary, "A Prayer Before Dying," November 29): "The U.S. has a long investigation to finish before it can prove any hypothesis is valid. It took investigators 16 months to conclude effectively that an exploded fuel tank, not a missile, brought down TWA 800. The truth about EgyptAir 990 still lies hidden in the deep."

[Michael J. Sniffen reported ("EgyptAir Probe Focusing on Tape," *AP*, November 18, 1999), "A team of government safety experts, hired translators, and Egyptian, FBI and manufacturer representatives is trying to precisely transcribe EgyptAir 990's cockpit voice recorder tape,...The group will work all weekend and hopes to complete the transcript next week, the NTSB said Wednesday."]

[As of March 15, 2000, the transcript, expected to take five days, had not been released.]

November 30, 1999

Secret Evidence Used to Prosecute Arabs, Muslims

Nasser K. Ahmed, jailed by the U.S. government for more than three years on the basis of secret evidence was freed last night, but about 20 others remain in jail on the basis of a 1996 antiterrorism bill authorizing the use of secret evidence in deportation proceedings.

Ahmed's case is not yet over—he is free on personal bond pending a final ruling by the Immigration and Naturalization Service, Board of Immigration Appeals on whether he should be granted asylum. Using secret evidence, that is evidence not shown to the accused, the INS had sought to deport Ahmed to Egypt after he overstayed his visa.

Ahmed was accused of belonging to an Egyptian terrorist group of which Abdel Rahman is said to be the spiritual leader. Ahmed admitted to being an admirer of Sheikh Abdel Rahman, but has denied involvement in terrorism.

Ahmed's release came 40 days after that of Hany Kiareldeen, a 32-year-old Palestinian immigrant, who had been held by the INS since March 1998 because the FBI's Joint Terrorism Task Force had developed secret evidence that he had hosted a meeting with terrorists planning the World Trade Center bombing, and had talked of murdering Attorney General Janet Reno.

Immigration judge, Donn Livingston, sharply criticized the government's case, calling it "double or triple hearsay," and questioned the reliability of some government sources, saying he had a "very real concern" that the Egyptian government might be the source of secret evidence against Ahmed. Judge Livingston cited "the very real danger that the Egyptian government" was seeking to silence Abdel Rahman, one of its harshest critics reports Benjamin Weiser of the *New York Times* ("U.S. Frees Egyptian Jailed on Secret Evidence," November 30, 1999).

The U.S. government also sought to use secret evidence to expel six Iraqis brought to this country by the CIA. In another case, the government arrested and sought to deport eight Los Angeles activists for the Popular Front for the Liberation of Palestine on the basis of secret evidence.

The use of secret evidence by the INS was first authorized by the

1996 antiterrorism bill that followed the World Trade Center and Oklahoma City bombings. Secret evidence has been used in about two dozen cases around the country in which the INS asserted national security concerns as the basis for depriving immigrants of the right to examine and confront adverse witnesses and evidence. All of the cases are against Arab or Muslim immigrants reported Lorraine Adams and David A. Vise of the *Washington Post* ("Classified Evidence Ruled Out in Deportation, October 21, 1999).

For the first time, on October 20, a federal court weighed the constitutionality of the use of secret evidence and found it unconstitutional.

Federal district Judge William Walls held in Kiareldeen's case that "the government's reliance on secret evidence violates the due process protections that the Constitution directs must be extended to all persons within the United States, citizens and resident aliens alike."

However, the 1996 antiterrorism bill has yet to be repealed or revised.

Representative David E. Bonior of Michigan has introduced legislation to ban the use of secret evidence in deportation proceedings. Says Rep. Bonior, "we still have about 20 others who are being held, and it's a travesty of justice that this continues in our country without people having the right to face their accusers."

December 6, 1999

Religion Newswriters Association Bashes Islam

"Top 10 Stories of The Millennium" includes event that never took place!

Among the top 10 stories of the millennium, according to the Religion Newswriters Association, is "Islam's expansion into Africa, Europe and Asia, including its move into India (1190-1200), resulting in the destruction of most of the subcontinent's indigenous Buddhist culture."

There's just one problem with this story. Islam did not destroy Buddhist culture. Buddhism never really caught on in India. It was absorbed into Hinduism.

It's worth reading what Pandit Jawaharlal Nehru said about Islam's expansion in "The Discovery of India." Pandit Nehru, together with Mahatma Gandhi, and Maulana Abul Kalam Azad led India's independence movement. Pandit Nehru, a Hindu, and India's first prime minister had this to say:

• Frequent intercourse [trade and cultural relations] led to Indians getting to know the religion, Islam. Missionaries also came to spread the new faith and they were welcomed. Mosques were built. There was no objection raised either by the state or the people, nor were there any religious conflicts.

• Mahmud's raids are a big event in Indian history....Above all they brought Islam, for the first time, to the accompaniment of ruthless military conquest. So far, for over 300 years, Islam had come peacefully as a religion and taken its place among the many religions of India without trouble or conflict....Yet when he [Mahmud] had established himself as a ruler...Hindus were appointed to high office in the army and the administration.

• It is thus wrong and misleading to think of a Muslim invasion of India or of the Muslim period in India, just as it would be wrong to refer to the coming of the British to India as a Christian invasion, or to call the British period in India a Christian period. Islam did not invade India; it had come to India some centuries earlier.

• As a warrior he [Akbar] conquered large parts of India, but his eyes were set on another and more enduring conquest, the conquest of the minds and hearts of the people...throughout his long reign of nearly fifty years from 1556 onwards he labored to that end.

Although Muslims ruled India for several centuries, Hinduism remains the dominant religion, and Sikhism, a new religion combining elements of Islam and Hinduism, was born. King Akbar even tried to form a new religion, Din Elahi, combining the best of several religions, but it attracted few followers.

Islam attracted a following in India for the same reasons that it did in North Africa.

Jawaharlal Nehru had this to say about Islam's spread: "North Africa was torn with internecine conflicts between rival Christian factions, leading often to bloody struggles for mastery. The Christianity that was practised there at the time was narrow and intolerant and the contrast between this and the general toleration of the Muslim Arabs, with their message of human brotherhood, was marked. It was this that brought whole peoples, weary of Christian strife, to their side."

Perhaps the most striking example of Islam's peaceful spread is Indonesia. The largest Muslim country, with more than 200 million people spread over 6,000 island, was never invaded by Muslims. Islam was spread by the example of traders.

The Hindu scholar, and noted historian, Dr. Bishambhar Nath Pande said, "History was compiled by European writers whose main objective was to produce histories that would serve their policy of divide and rule."

We're reminded of Dorothy Gilliam's column of December 20, 1997 for the *Washington Post*. Ms. Gilliam wrote, "Newsrooms that do not reflect America's diversity do their readers an injustice. They fail to tell the stories of its citizens, they give readers a distorted image of themselves and they grossly twist the reality of minority groups."

We asked Debra Mason, executive director, Religion Newswriters Association, where are the facts to support the statement that Islam's expansion into India resulted in "the destruction of most of the subcontinent's indigenous Buddhist culture?" Ms. Mason didn't respond.

December 7, 1999

Russia to Chechens: "Get Out or Die"

The deadline is this Saturday. Forty thousand Chechens trapped in Grozny have been delivered an ultimatum by Russia: "Get out or die." And the Russians may also be using chemical weapons.

A communique, received today by The Wisdom Fund, from Mr. Colin Archer, secretary-general of International Peace Bureau (IPB) states: "Russian forces are using chemical weapons in their attack on Grozny, declared three Chechen representatives at a meeting with journalists in Geneva this morning." The IPB is among the oldest of the international peace federations covering issues ranging from nuclear weapons and landmines to conflict resolution and peace education.

President Clinton has criticized the Russian ultimatum to civilians, calling it "a threat to the lives of the old, the infirm, the injured people, and other innocent civilians who simply cannot leave or are too scared to leave their homes."

But the Russians have shrugged off the West's belated criticism. Russia had earlier been given the green light for the attack on Chechnya by U.S. Secretary of State Madeleine Albright who dismissed proposals for cutting off aid to Russia.

BBC News Online reported (November 5) that Secretary Albright said the war in Chechnya must not be allowed to damage relations between Russia and the West, and turn Russia back into a Cold War enemy. Albright added, "We believe it is very important for there to be economic stability in Russia. That is in our national interest."

Russia launched this war on Chechnya in retaliation for alleged bombings of apartment buildings in Moscow. The Chechens deny they are responsible, and view the war as being prosecuted primarily to assure the election prospects of Russian prime minister Vladimir Putin.

"Russian parliamentary elections are scheduled for December 19, and the results are regarded as a bellwether for next year's presidential vote. Putin has staked his presidential candidacy on the war's outcome, and so far his popularity has soared" (Daniel Williams, "Russia Tells Chechens: Leave Grozny or Die," *The Washington Post*, December 7).

For Russia and the West the fate of the Chechens, who have suffered 250 years of brutal, colonial rule, is overshadowed by "The Great Game"—a reference to the rivalry between Imperial Russia and the British Empire over influence in Central Asia at the end of the last century—being replayed.

Thomas Goltz, author of *Azerbaijan Diary: A Rogue Reporter's Adventures in an Oil-rich, War-Torn, Post-Soviet Republic* due this winter, writes, "This time the stakes are just as high—control over the vast deposits of "sweet" crude oil beneath the Caspian Sea—but there are more players. The United States (and the West) is taking a keen interest in the region as an alternative source of energy supply for the next century. Russia has long regarded the Caspian as its strategic reserve and

Moscow does not take kindly to the prospect of the once-Soviet states which actually sit on the oil drilling their way to real economic independence.

Goltz adds, "Iran is keenly interested both in becoming a player itself and in keeping the United States from dominating its backyard to the North. Turkey desperately seeks a sphere of influence of its own after being effectively locked out of the European Union. Even China, the new giant Tiger to the East, has indicated interest."

Michael T. Klare, professor of peace and world security studies at Hampshire College in Amherst, Massachusetts, and the author of the forthcoming book, *Resource Wars: Global Geopolitics in the 21st Century* writes: "Now, in this new era of geopolitical competition, Clinton wants the oil to move along an east-west axis from Turkmenistan to Azerbaijan (this part traversing the Caspian Sea itself) and thence by land to Georgia and Turkey, thereby avoiding both Russia and Iran.

The agreement signed by Turkmenistan, Azerbaijan, Georgia and Turkey on November 18th in Istanbul achieves president Clinton's key objective, and raises the stakes for Russia.

December 31, 1999

Facts Belie Hype about "Islamic Terrorism"

This decade ended with the media hyping "Islamic terrorism," while mass murder of Muslims goes unpunished, and in the guise of helping Muslims, their countries are exploited. Just review what's been happening in Bosnia, Chechnya, Indonesia, Kosovo, and the Middle East.

In *Patterns of Global Terrorism: 1998*, the U.S. Department of State says, "the number of international terrorist attacks actually fell again in 1998, continuing a downward trend that began several years ago." But media hype about terrorism, and the budget for the war against terrorism has been on an upward trend.

According to the State Department report, the "Total International Attacks by Region" are as follows:

Total International Attacks by Region

	1993	1994	1995	1997	1997	1998
Africa	6	25	10	11	11	21
Asia	37	24	16	11	21	49
Eurasia	5	11	5	24	42	14
Latin America	97	58	92	84	128	110
Middle East	100	116	45	45	37	31
North America	1	0	0	0	13	0
West Europe	185	88	272	121	52	48

Other useful statistics from the Department of State report, the "Total U.S. Citizen Casualties Caused by International Attacks," are as follows:

Total U.S. Citizen Casualties Caused by International Attacks

	1993	1994	1995	1997	1997	1998
Dead	7	6	10	25	6	12
Wounded	1004	5	60	510	21	11

Perhaps, the more interesting statistics, as far as "Islamic terrorism" is concerned, appear in "Total Anti-U.S. Attacks," which lists attacks by region as follows: Africa—3, Europe—3, West Europe—13, Middle East—5, and Latin America—87.

From these statistics, it is evident that Americans have little to fear from terrorism in the U.S., and even less from "Islamic terrorism." And, given the statistics for the Middle East and Latin America, one wonders why one doesn't hear about "Christian terrorism," at least as often as one hears about "Islamic terrorism."

Furthermore, according to John Mueller and Karl Mueller ("Sanctions of Mass Destruction," *Foreign Affairs*, May/June 1999), "On average far fewer Americans are killed each year by terrorists than are killed by lightning, deer accidents, or peanut allergies. To call terrorism a threat to national security is scarcely plausible." The Muellers add, "Economic sanctions may well have been a necessary cause of the deaths of more people in Iraq than have been slain by all so-called weapons of mass destruction throughout history."

Graham E. Fuller, former vice chairman of the National Intelligence Council at the CIA, says ("Airstrikes Aren't the Endgame," *Los*

Angeles Times, August 24, 1998), "it is dangerous to divorce terrorism from politics, yet the U.S. media continue to talk about an abstract war against terrorism without mention of the issues or context that lie behind them."

["If the agenda can be restricted to the ambiguities of Arafat, the abuses and failures of the Sandinistas, the terrorism of Iran and Libya, and other properly framed issues, then the game is basically over; excluded from the discussion is the unambiguous rejectionism of the United States and Israel, and the terrorism and other crimes of the United States and its clients, not only far greater in scale but also incomparably more significant on any moral dimension for American citizens, who are in a position to mitigate or terminate these crimes."—Noam Chomsky, *Necessary Illusions,* p. 49]

[Iraq's invasion of Kuwait took about 360 lives. According to the documentary *Panama Deception*—produced by the Empowerment Project and broadcast in more than 20 countries worldwide, Blue Ribbon winner at the American Film & Video Festival in 1993, and recipient of several international film awards—the U.S. invasion of Panama, to capture Gen. Noriega, took about 3,000 lives.]

January 8, 2000

Chechens Pay for Putin's Rise, Yeltsin's Immunity

The Chechens are paying a high price for Mr. Vladimir Putin's rise from obscurity to Acting President of Russia, and for his grant of immunity to former president Boris Yeltsin who was being investigated on charges of corruption.

A series of bomb explosions last summer in Moscow and other Russian cities was the beginning of Putin's rise to power and popularity. According to Stephen Mulvey, until his appointment as Prime Minister last August ("Vladimir Putin: Spy Turned Politician," *BBC News Online*, January 1, 2000), "he was a little known figure who had spent most of his career working for the Soviet security service, the KGB, including several years as a spy in Germany. In a matter of weeks he had become the most popular politician in the country, and by the end of the year, the acting president."

According to the *Economist* (Editorial, January 8, 2000), "No clear evidence has yet been found for who was responsible for those bombs, and no one has claimed responsibility." But, says the *Economist*, given the huge benefits that Putin, and the security forces in general, have gained from those tragedies it would be foolish to rule out Putin's role in the bombing.

The *Independent* (Helen Womack, "Russian Agents 'Blew Up Moscow Flats'," January 6, 2000) has obtained a videotape in which a Russian officer, Lieutenant Galtin, captured at the border between Dagestan and Chechnya while on a mine-laying mission says, "I know who is responsible for the bombings in Moscow (and Dagestan). It is the FSB (Russian security service), in cooperation with the GRU, that is responsible for the explosions in Volgodonsk and Moscow."

This confirms what Dr. Aslambek Kadiev told BBC ("A Chechen View of Russia's War," December 26, 1999) a few days earlier. Said Dr. Aslambek, "There are two main reasons for the two wars which Russia has launched against Chechnya. The first is economic: Russia wants to control the Caucasus oil fields and pipeline routes. The second is connected with the political situation in Russia, and particularly inside the Kremlin."

Dr. Kadiev explains, "The political purpose of the first Chechen war was to increase Boris Yeltsin's popularity and get him reelected president in 1996. The main aim of this second war is to ensure that Prime Minister Vladimir Putin, a former spy and President Yeltsin's anointed heir, becomes president at the next elections. The apartment bombings in Russian cities early this year were used by Russia to justify its invasion."

Boris Yeltsin stunned Russians by announcing his resignation, and saying elections for a new president will be held in 90 days. According to the *Associated Press* (Barry Renfrew, "Yeltsin Resigns, Turns Over Powers," January 31, 1999), "Yeltsin said he was stepping down immediately because he wanted Prime Minister Vladimir Putin to succeed him. Putin then signed a decree offering Yeltsin immunity from prosecution, a lifetime pension, a government country home and bodyguards and medical care for him and his family."

According to the *Washington Post* (Sharon LaFraniere, "Yeltsin is Linked to Bribe Scheme," September 8, 1999), a Swiss investigation uncovered evidence that "a construction company that received major

Kremlin contracts paid tens of thousands of dollars of bills charged to credit cards in the names of Russian President Boris Yeltsin and his two daughters," Yelena Okulova and Tatyana Dyachenko. And this may be just the tip of the iceberg.

About $100 billion to $150 billion has fled abroad since 1992, according to Russian and Western estimates (David Hoffman, "Russia's Cash Flow Flows Out," *Washington Post*, August 29,1999). "Russian general prosecutor, Yuri Skuratov, had threatened to reveal the identities of what he described as high-level government officials with Swiss bank accounts. They had been examining how the foreign currency earnings of the national airline, Aeroflot, were reportedly channeled into a Swiss company believed by the investigators to be controlled by tycoon Boris Berezovsky."

As long as he remained in office, Yeltsin was immune from prosecution. But with presidential elections scheduled for next May, Yeltsin had three choices: flee the country, choose a sympathetic successor, or declare a state of emergency, canceling the elections. Vladimir Putin, his handpicked successor, granted immunity and more to Boris Yeltsin.

The Chechens, who are paying with their lives for the Yeltsin/Putin *Wag the Dog* war, have endured 250 years of brutal Russian occupation. About one-quarter of them perished during forced exile by Stalin in 1944. Since the recent Russian war on Chechnya, an estimated 200,000 Chechen refugees have fled to Ingushetia. About 3,000 have been killed, and 10,000 wounded. And 40,000 remain trapped in basements in Chechnya in subfreezing temperatures.

Now, according to the London *Times* (Alice Lagnado, January 8, 2000), "Russia may resort to more powerful weapons to end a war that is going badly. Vacuum bombs could bring the fighting to a speedy end. Russian forces may also be considering the use of chemical weapons."

The U.S. attitude to the war in Chechnya was summed up in statements by Madeleine Albright, and Lawrence Eagleburger.

Said the Canadian columnist, Eric Margolis ("U.S. Aids Russia's Crimes in the Caucasus," *Toronto Sun*, October 12, 1999), "In Moscow, standing next to her beaming Russians hosts, US Secretary of State Madeleine Albright proclaimed 'we are opposed to terrorism'—meaning Islamic rebels in the Caucasus fighting Russian rule. She said nothing about Russia's blatant violation of its 1996 treaty that granted Chechnya de facto independence. She made no protest over Moscow's egregious violation of the 1990 CFE [Conventional Forces in Europe] Treaty, the most important east-west arms reduction pact, by moving large new forces into the Caucasus."

And on a recent PBS "Newshour with Jim Lehrer," former U.S. Secretary of State Lawrence Eagleburger rationalized Russia's genocidal war on Chechnya, saying, "They're not very nice people."

[Former Russian prime minister, Mr. Sergei Stepashin, in recent interviews with the daily *Nezavissimaya Gazeta* and Interfax agency, said the plan to send the Russian army into Chechnya 'had been worked out in March.' He says he played a central role in organizing the military build up before the invasion, which 'had to happen even if there were no explosions in Moscow.'"—Patrick Cockburn, "Russia planned Chechen war before bombings," *Independent*, January 29, 2000]

[The U.S. reaction is apparent from the following: Sharon LaFraniere, "Allbright Hails Putin's Can-Do Style," *Washington Post*, February 3, 2000]

January 15, 2000

Media Show Bias in Coverage of Violence in Indonesia

The U.S. media's anti-Muslim bias shows once again in their reports on the violence in Indonesia, where calls of "jihad" receive widespread newspaper and television coverage, but the massacre and burning of dozens of Muslims by Christians—the reason for the call to "jihad"—gets little or no coverage.

Richard Lloyd Parry, Asia Correspondent for the *Independent*, reported on January 11, 2000 that, "Aid workers say they have found the bodies of large numbers of Muslims massacred and burnt by Christians in the ongoing violence in the Indonesian Spice Islands."

Mr. Parry reports, "A doctor with the aid team said he had seen a mosque in the village of Popilo in which bodies lay five deep. More bodies, including those of young children, were bulldozed into the ground near by. 'I think it was about 200 bodies,' he was quoted as saying. 'I saw some dried blood in the mosque, so I assume...that the victims were slaughtered inside the mosque.'"

On January 5, 2000, Irwin Firdaus of the *Associated Press* had written, "Media reports in Jakarta said up to 10,000 people on Halmahera [in the Spice Islands] were seeking shelter in military barracks while waiting to be evacuated. The *Indonesian Observer* daily quoted local residents as saying most of those fleeing were Muslim, and that Christian militias had gone on a killing spree throughout the island."

Yet, as far as we can tell, this Christian killing spree was not covered by U.S. media. Instead U.S. media paid far greater attention to Muslims calling for "jihad" in the Indonesian capital, Jakarta.

They did not report why Muslims were calling for "jihad," nor the various meanings of jihad (or struggle), thereby, leaving the impression of a bloodthirsty Muslim majority out to kill Christians—just because they are Christian.

The truth is considerably more complex, and neither Muslims nor Christians are blameless.

The 1000 plus islands comprising the Moluccas (or Maluku) in Indonesia, stretch from Halmahera in the north to Wetar off the northeastern end of Timor. The largest of the islands, Halmahera and Seram, are the most undeveloped and underpopulated. The smallest, Ambon and the Bandas, are the most developed and populated.

The Moluccas—the fabled Spice Islands—to which Indians, Chinese, Arabs, and Europeans came in search of cloves, nutmeg, and mace, bore the brunt of the first European attempts to colonize Indonesia.

The Portuguese were the first to arrive in 1509, followed by the Dutch in 1599. By 1630 the Dutch were established in Ambon, and they had established their headquarters in Jakarta.

After a brief occupation by the British, the Dutch returned in 1814, but encountered resistance. The leader of the rebellion, Pattimura, was captured and executed. He is regarded as one of Indonesia's national heroes—Ambon's university and airport are named after him.

When the Dutch left Indonesia after World War II, the mainly Christian population of Ambon in the Moluccas, proclaimed an independent Republic of the South Moluccas (Republic Maluku Selatan; RMS) rather than join with the rest of mainly Muslim Indonesia.

In 1950 Indonesian troops occupied the islands, and the Ambonese, many of whom worked for the Dutch, as missionaries or soldiers in the Dutch army, fled to the jungles of Seram.

The Dutch intended to demobilize them, and send them back to Ambon. But fearing that this would mean sending them to their death, about 12,000 were taken to the Netherlands by the Dutch government. And from the Netherlands they continue their resistance to Indonesian rule. Many have returned to retire or do business.

The violence in the Moluccas has come amid increasing religious tensions, fueled in part by Muslim migration to the islands, which during Dutch rule had a Christian majority.

Adding to the religious tensions is the prospect of wealth for some.

According to *AFP* (January 11, 2000), Indonesian president, Abdurrahman Wahid, said that the most recent bloody Muslim-Christian battles on Halmahera island in North Maluku, which have left hundreds killed, were "perpetrated by someone who wants to be the governor of the province," as well as "the prospect of a gold mine" in the area.

Others, rumored to be after the oil on Seram, may be fueling the violence which has taken about 2,000 lives in the past year.

["Audi Wuisan, the coordinator of the crisis center of the Indonesian Council of Churches,...said on January 13, copies of an open letter had circulated in West Nusatenggara province, of which Lombok is part, telling Christians there to condemn Christians in Maluku for slaughtering 3,000 Muslims."—"Angry Indonesian Mob Sets Churches on Fire over Slaughter of Muslims," *AFP*, January 17, 2000]

["A Muslim mob set fire today to at least eight churches on the Indonesian tourist island of Lombok and battled police trying to stop the spread of religious violence that has claimed more than 2,000 lives....On Saturday, the Indonesian Council of Ulamas, a powerful group of Islamic leaders, said it supported calls for a holy war to protect Muslims from any further violence."—Ali Kotarumalos, "Indonesian Religious Violence Grows," *AP*, January 17, 2000. Note: The *AP* version of the same incident, does not mention the slaughter of 3000 Muslims reported by *AFP*. It does mention "2000 lives" claimed by violence, but does not say whose lives were taken. Given the references to "holy war," American readers are likely to assume that it is Christian lives that were taken, in mostly Muslim Indonesia.]

[On January 24, 2000, about 200 hospital staff, 700 patients and visitors were taken hostage in Thailand by the Christian fundamentalist God's Army. On January 25, an *AP* headline read, "Myanmar Hostage Takers Were Polite." Compare news coverage with that of Muslims.]

January 21, 2000,

Toward Justice and Peace

President George Bush, reports *Agence France-Presse*, January 19, 2000, said to U.S. soldiers in the ongoing Gulf War—in words reminiscent of previous colonial empire-builders—that they were "doing God's work." Mr. George Kennan, who headed the U.S. Department of State planning staff until 1950, phrased it more honestly.

In 1948, when developing countries were beginning to emerge from Western colonial rule, Kennan "the leading dove and peace prize winner," in the top secret, U.S. Department of State, Policy Planning Study 23, prescribed in part: "We have about 50% of the world's wealth, but only 6.3% of its population....Our real task in the coming period is to devise a pattern of relationships which will permit us to maintain this position of disparity....To do so, we will have to dispense with all sentimentality. ...We should cease to talk about vague and...unreal objectives such as human rights, the raising of living standards, and democratization."

More simply stated, Kennan's prescription was: follow the money. It appears that Kennan's prescription for U.S. foreign policy remains the guiding light. This, President Bush wouldn't want to tell the American people.

Security, as it should be, is at the heart of U.S. policy. But far too many decisions are rationalized as being security driven, when it is greed that is the determining force. The Gulf War of 1991 is an outstanding example. It was fought for control of Middle East resources, not for U.S. security.

Geographically, the U.S. is among the most secure land masses. Yet it continues to outspend, by several orders of magnitude, all potential adversaries combined.

The $284 billion U.S. defense budget is over 10 times that of Russia, China and India combined, about 20 times that of all the "rogue states," and about 100 times that of Iraq. The U.S.'s $30 billion spending for covert operations alone is twice the total defense spending of the so-called "rogue states."

Add to U.S. defense spending, the defense spending of U.S. allies (over $120 billion annually), and the figures get even more distorted. When the U.S. and its allies—armed forces with annual spending of $387 billion—attacked Yugoslavia, they faced an enemy that spent less than one billion annually.

It is the magnitude of defense spending that fuels the search for enemies.

In this decade, with the collapse of the Soviet Union, the choice was between the Yellow Peril (East Asia) and the Green Peril (Islam). Islam was chosen. And Iran, Iraq, Libya, Syria were designated "rogue states." These were joined by Cuba, North Korea, and Sudan.

While these states may have engaged in terrorism, and other unsavory activities, they weren't doing anything that the U.S. had not done, and was doing. Using the same criteria applied to the "rogue states," it is difficult not to conclude that the U.S. itself is a rogue state, and so are England, Russia, and others.

Since the fall of the Soviet Union, at least $500 billion of unnecessary funding went to fight the bogey of "Islamic fundamentalism." Despite this, in 1996 President Clinton added $124 billion to defense and cut $55 billion from welfare.

The U.S. speaks of democracy, human rights, and free trade, but these are merely slogans to coerce weaker nations to submit to exploitation by the West. The absence of democracy and human rights does not deter U.S. relations with another country, and it is not free trade that the U.S. seeks, but capitalism—the latter seeks to eliminate free trade not foster it.

Capitalism is but a variation on the British East India Company which held monopoly rights to extract the wealth of overseas colonies. Today's version of the British East India Company are large oil companies, mining companies, private power producers, etc. Indeed, capitalism, unchecked, destroys the very conditions that generations of economists such as Adam Smith have found to be essential to an efficient market— a market composed solely of individual buyers and sellers, none large enough to influence the market price.

The world's 48 poorest countries account for only 0.4 percent of world trade and their share is shrinking. The 1998 United Nations Human Development Report notes that in 1960 the income of the 20 percent of the world's people who lived in the richest countries was 30 times the income of the 20 percent who lived in the poorest countries. By 1995 the ratio was 82 to 1.

The spread of free-market reforms in Latin America failed to create enough new jobs to counter high unemployment rates caused by privatization and downsizing, and it increased the gap between rich and poor. The UN report says that in 100 countries, per capita income is actually lower now than it was 30 years ago.

Privatization created millionaires in Russia, while the vast majority of its citizens received even less than they had under the communist regime. Large, unregulated capital flows caused the near collapse of Malaysia and Indonesia. By following the prescription of its foreign advisors, Saudi Arabia saw its per capita income drop from $15,700 in 1980, to $5,700 today. In 1982, Saudi Arabia had reserves of $170 billion. Today, the national debt is almost that amount.

The U.S. speaks of its war on terrorism, but it is U.S. intervention in the affairs of other states that provokes retaliation and keeps the dollars flowing to the arms manufacturers. So the war on terrorism goes on. Again, greed is the driving force.

Meanwhile, major media inundate us with half truths, sometimes outright lies. Their propaganda is designed to divide the masses, when the common enemy is those who exploit the masses. Of course, since the media itself is owned by a very small number of large corporations its loyalty to them is understandable.

But there have also been positive developments.

This decade has seen the rise of hundreds of organizations, thousands of individuals—Jews, Christians, Muslims, and others—working for a just and peaceful world.

The Internet has brought unprecedented power to the masses. Its potential has just begun to be exploited. Given a willingness to cooperate and communicate, and with common purpose, much can be accomplished.

The masses everywhere have much in common. They value survival, family, friends in roughly that order. Those with greater means look toward helping others, saving the environment. And to some degree they search for something beyond all of that to find satisfaction in creating, in self-growth, in spiritual pursuit.

The war on Islam, backed by a foreign policy establishment subservient to the Zionists, is being waged not because of differences in matters of faith, but because vast resources are to be had in Muslim lands, because the U.S. needs an enemy to justify defense spending, and perhaps even more importantly because Islam's prescription for a just social order opposes Kennan's prescription.

Kennan's prescription leads to unbridled capitalism, and exploitation of the masses. Islam's prescription for a just social order opposes unbridled capitalism, supports free markets, and cannot be overturned by legislation or executive order.

The war on Islam has about as much to do with faith as did the wars waged by the Europeans after the fall of Muslim Spain in 1492.

John Edwards, in *History Today* wrote: "On the second day of January [1492] I saw Your Highnesses' royal banners placed by force of arms on the towers of the Alhambra...and in the same month...Your Highness, as Catholic Christians and princes devoted to the holy Christian faith and the furtherance of its cause, and enemies of the sect of Mohammed and of all idolatry and heresy, resolved to send me, Christopher Columbus, to the...regions of India."

We now know that for Columbus, and the Europeans who came after him, the primary driving force was not that they were "devoted to the holy Christian faith and the furtherance of its cause." They raped, pillaged, murdered for gold, diamonds, and other wealth. Columbus may have embarked upon his first voyage for the joy of discovery, but soon greed became the driving force. Uncounted millions were enslaved or died to satisfy that greed.

Soon other Europeans with similar desires spread across the Americas, Africa, Asia, Australia, and China bringing with them slavery, death, destruction. Greed drove them on.

Greed is the determining force today for those who seek to exploit the resources of the Middle East, the Caspian Sea, Indonesia. Islam is portrayed as the enemy to convince Americans, Europeans, and Russians that war is necessary.

Under the guise of saving humanity, and preserving civil society, the U.S.-led NATO is assaulting the world—causing death, destruction and misery. Little has changed since 1492, except the technology for fighting wars, and for demonizing the "enemy."

With the demise of the Soviet Union, the U.S. had an opportunity to create a "New World Order" based upon justice and peace. Instead, U.S. military ventures from Iraq to the former Yugoslavia, in pursuit of an insatiable desire for wealth, has reignited the Cold War, and set precedents likely to lead to more wars.

Russia's genocidal attack on Chechnya is the result. And what little there was of world order, such as international law and the United Nations, is being deliberately trampled upon.

With enough people dedicated to justice and peace, wars can be stopped. The people did it in the 1960s with the Viet Nam war. Awakened from apathy, they can do it again. The demonstrations at the World Trade Organization conference in Seattle may mark the beginning of this new awakening.

While the biased reporting of U.S. media remains the biggest obstacle, it also presents the biggest opportunity for concerned Americans to move the U.S. toward policies likely to lead to enduring peace.

With some exceptions, the real war is neither a war between different faiths, nor different races, nor different states. It is a war between those driven by greed, and those seeking justice and peace. As long as the those driven by greed seek ever greater resources and markets, or to control those resources and markets, the rest are likely to suffer. And it is the latter who are most likely to die in wars, while those who lead them into war reap the spoils of victory.

When enough people realize that the war on Islam is ultimately a clash of values—greed versus justice, mercy, compassion—we may be closer to a new world order which leads us toward justice and peace.

❖

As we enter the New Millennium:

U.S. media continues its
jihad against Islam.

Five thousand Iraqis die each month
due to sanctions enforced by the U.S.

Peace remains an elusive dream in
Chechnya, the Middle East,
 and other Muslim lands.

The "Great Game" is not over.

Appendix

Selected Bibliography

Introduction to Islam

Sir Abdullah Suhrawardy, *The Sayings of Muhammad*—Gandhi referred to these sayings as "the treasures of mankind." This introduction to Islamic values was found in the overcoat pocket of Leo Tolstoy when he took his last walk in the fields he used to till.

Roger Du Pasquier, *Unveiling Islam*—Swiss journalist and winner of the 1988 French Authors' Association prize reports, "The West...has never really known Islam. Ever since they watched it appear on the world stage, Christians never ceased to insult and slander it in order to find justifications for waging war on it."

Martin Lings, *Muhammad: His Life Based on the Earliest Sources*—Based upon the words of men and women who heard Muhammad speak and witnessed the events of his life, this is acclaimed worldwide as the definitive biography of the Prophet in the English language.

Akbar S. Ahmed, *Living Islam*—Basis for a BBC television series; good overview of Islam's past and present; nicely illustrated.

Feisal Abdul Rauf, *Islam: A Sacred Law*—With intellect, common sense, and wit, Imam Feisal applies traditional law to contemporary issues and moral dilemmas.

Howard R. Turner, *Science in Medieval Islam: An Illustrated Introduction*—Describes Islam's achievements, and contributions to, mathematics, astronomy, physics, medicine, and more.

Maurice Bucaille, *The Bible, the Qur'an and Science*—An examination of the confrontation between the Bible and scientific data leads us to meditate upon those factors which should spiritually unite rather than divide Jews, Christians, and Muslims.

Charles Le Gai Eaton, *Islam and the Destiny of Man*—As a British diplomat who converted to Islam, Mr. Eaton is unique in his ability to convey some of the more complicated aspects of Islam in a comprehensive and palatable manner to the Western reader.

Introduction to U.S. History and Politics

Howard Zinn, *Declarations of Independence: Cross-Examining American Ideology*—Professor of history and political science, former air force bombardier in Europe, presents conclusions which challenge establishment myths.

John Pilger, *Hidden Agendas*—Journalist, twice winner of Britain's Journalist of the Year award, gives the unfiltered truth about worldwide struggles for justice and the veiled role of the U.S. and Britain.

Chalmers A. Johnson, *Blowback: The Costs & Consequences of American Empire*—If the 20th century was the American century, the 21st century may be a time of reckoning for the United States.

William Blum, *Killing Hope: US Military and CIA Interventions Since World War II*—Is the United States a force for democracy? From China in the 1940s to Guatemala to the Gulf War, former U.S. Dept. of State official provides a comprehensive study of the ongoing American holocaust.

Paul Findley, *Deliberate Deceptions*—U.S. Representative from Illinois speaks out on the facts behind the U.S.-Israeli relationship, and they're not what establishment media generally report.

Deirdre Griswold, *Indonesia : The 2nd Greatest Crime of the Century*—Describes 350 years of colonialism, the blood bath supported by the U.S., the role of the CIA, and of the U.S. corporations who arrived for the feast.

Michael Klare, *Rogue States and Nuclear Outlaws*—Pentagon manufactured threat of rogue states and nuclear outlaws to protect cold war levels of defense spending which former Defense Secretary McNamara says could safely be cut in half.

Ramsey Clark, *The Fire This Time: U.S. Crimes in the Gulf*—Former U.S. Attorney General says that the U.S. government bears prime responsibility for the Gulf War which was planned in Washington long before the first Iraqi soldier entered Kuwait.

Bruce B. Lawrence, *Shattering the Myth: Islam Beyond Violence*—Islam's portrayal in Western media, as an alien, violent, hostile religion more accurately reflects the bias of Western reporters than they do the realities of Islam.

Larry J. Sabato and Glenn R. Simpson, *Dirty Little Secrets : The Persistence of Corruption in American Politics*—Four out of five Americans don't trust their government. Authors describe the corruption in American politics, and what Americans should know if they are to reform the system.

Edward W. Said, *Covering Islam*—Columbia University professor reveals the hidden agendas and distortions of fact that underlie even the most "objective" coverage of the Islamic world.

J. M. Roberts, *The Penguin History of the World*—Provides a one volume outline of world history beginning with the origins of man. It is a sanitized yet less than admirable version of 500 years of Europe's exploitation of the world beginning with the fall of Muslim Spain in 1492.

Howard Zinn, *A People's History of the United States*—Describes the reality of 500 years of American democracy, capitalism, human rights, and the treatment of women, poor white Americans, Native Americans, and African Americans.

Noam Chomsky, *Deterring Democracy*—Reveals a world in which the U.S. ruthlessly exploits its financial and military might to control markets and resources—from Nicaragua to the Philippines, Panama to the Middle East.

Noam Chomsky, *The Culture of Terrorism*—"U.S. international and security policy...has as its primary goal...the freedom to rob, to exploit and dominate, and to undertake any course of action to ensure that existing privilege is protected and enhanced.

John Tirman, *The Spoils of War: Human Cost of America's Arms Trade*—Executive Director of the Winston Foundation, writes that the Middle East conflict is the direct result of US arms sales to the region, and such sales undermine the very security that the weapons were meant to protect.

Graham Hancock, *Lords of Poverty: The Power, Prestige, and Corruption of the International Aid Business*—A comprehensive study of the 60 billion dollar a year world foreign aid business. Lords of Poverty earned the 1990 H. L. Mencken Award honorable mention for an outstanding book of journalism.

Robert Tillman, Kitty Calavita, Henry N. Pontell, *Big Money Crime: Fraud and Politics in the Savings and Loan Crisis*—Authors describe white collar crimes, unparalleled in US history, that cost the taxpayer $500 billion. The BCCI scandal of 1991, and the collapse of SE Asia's economy in 1997, pale in comparison.

William Greider, *Secrets of the Temple: How the Federal Reserve Runs the Country*—Reveals for the first time how the mighty and mysterious Federal Reserve actually operates, and how it manipulated and transformed both America's economy and the world's.

William Greider, *Who Will Tell the People: The Betrayal of American Democracy*—A bestselling exposé of political power and public deception that reveals a government that ignores popular will and responds instead to the interests of major organizations and influential elites.

Charles Derber, *The Wilding of America*—Capitalism and individualism run amok are destroying America, and creating a world in which multinationals control national governments.

Edward S. Herman, Noam Chomsky, *Manufacturing Consent: The Political Economy of the Mass Media*—As an analysis of press censorship in the U.S., it is an insightful look at the ways public opinion and choices are molded by dominating interests.

Gerry Spence, *Give Me Liberty!*—Celebrated attorney offers a revolutionary agenda for freeing Americans from the complex web of corporate and government behemoths that he calls the "New Slave Master."

Roger Garaudy, *The Founding Myths of Israeli Politics*—One of Europe's top Marxist thinkers for decades before his conversion to Islam, now 85 and on trial for writing this book, claims there exists a Zionist/media conspiracy to control the foreign policy of the US and France.

[Most of these books may be purchased through The Wisdom Fund web site—www.twf.org]

Realpolitik and Terrorism

Webster's New World Dictionary
Realpolitik—practical politics; a euphemism for power politics
power politics—international political relations in which each nation attempts to increase its own power or interests by using military or economic coercion
terrorism—1. the act of terrorizing; use of force or threats to demoralize, intimidate, and subjugate, esp. such use as a political weapon or policy 2. the demoralization and intimidation produced in this way
[Realpolitik = power politics = terrorism ?]

United States Senator Barry Goldwater
"Extremism in the pursuit of liberty is no vice. Moderation in the pursuit of justice is no virtue."

General Henry H. Shelton, Chairman of the Joint Chiefs of Staff, *60 Minutes*, April 30, 1995
The special forces are used "to put down rebellions or to start one."
[At the time, Gen. Shelton was head of a U.S. special forces unit.]

Ivan Eland, "Does U.S. Intervention Overseas Breed Terrorism?"
"According to the Pentagon's Defense Science Board, a strong correlation exists between U.S. involvement in international situations and an increase in terrorist attacks against the United States."
[Ivan Eland is director of defense policy studies at the Cato Institute.]

Stephen Endicott and Edward Hagerman, *The United States and Biological Warfare*
"The United States developed biological weapons and tested them on the North Koreans and the Chinese during the Korean War—outbreaks of cholera and plague in China are linked to American aerial attacks."

Peter Dale Scott, "U.S. Responsibility for the Slaughters"
"The massacres we do not hear about, at least at the time, are those for which the United States itself is responsible. This on-going, system-

atic suppression, from the Philippines in the 1950s to El Salvador in the 1980s, falsifies our understanding, not just of our own history, but of all managed atrocities throughout the world."

Noam Chomsky, *What Uncle Sam Really Wants*
"The use of terror is deeply ingrained in our [U.S.] character. The first step is to use the police. If major surgery becomes necessary, we rely on the army. When we can no longer control the army...it's time to overthrow the government. The second step is to use the military. The U.S. has always tried to establish relations with the military in foreign countries, because that's one of the ways to overthrow a government that has gotten out of hand."

"Wielding Aid, U.S. Targets Sudan," *Washington Post,* November 10, 1996
"Nearly $20 million in surplus U.S. military equipment will be sent to Ethiopia, Eritrea and Uganda, the officials said, adding that the three countries support Sudanese opposition groups preparing a joint offensive to topple the government of Sudan."
[If Sudan were to fund groups trying to "topple the government" of the U.S., would Sudan be supporting terrorism?]

"America to Fund Arms for Iraqi Rebels," *The Independent,* October 16, 1998
"The bill allocating $97m worth of military equipment to the Iraqi opposition was forced on the administration by Congress." Laith Kubba, an Iraqi intellectual, said: "The only result of this will be to turn Iraq into another Lebanon, with the development of militias armed by foreign powers in the name of democracy."

William Blum, *Killing Hope*
"While many nations have a terrible record in modern times of dealing out great suffering face-to-face with their victims, Americans have made it a point to keep at a distance while inflicting some of the greatest horrors of the age: atomic bombs on the people of Japan; carpet-bombing Korea back to the stone age; engulfing the Vietnamese in napalm and pesticides; providing three decades of Latin Americans with the tools and methods of torture, then turning their eyes away, closing

their ears to the screams, and denying everything ... and now, dropping 177 million pounds of bombs on the people of Iraq in the most concentrated aerial onslaught in the history of the world."

Phillipe Delmas, *The Rosy Future of War*
"The same Europe that we are now trumpeting as a model of pacifism has been built by wars, down to the last stone....The two World Wars—only recently fought—caused 100,000,000 deaths including 60,000,000 civilians. The Russian and Chinese Revolutions caused at least 50,000,000 more deaths; actually, historians have recently revised this upward to 100,000,000. As for the 146 little wars since 1945, they have discreetly exterminated close to 30,000,000 people, three-quarters of them civilians, and most of them in the name of the world powers....China has endured Western colonialism, invasion by the Japanese, liberation, and successive Maoist revolution: all told, China has suffered an estimated 30,000,000 to 60,000,000 deaths."

Roger Garaudy, *The Founding Myths of Israeli Politics*
"Hitlerism was a human catastrophe which, unfortunately, had a precedent in the policy applied over five centuries by the European colonialists to 'colored people.' What Hitler did to white people, they did to the American Indians, of which they killed [75%] (also through forced labor and epidemics, even more than through massacres); just as they did to the Africans, of which they deported between 10 and 20 million, which means that Africa was robbed of 100 to 200 million of its inhabitants since ten people had to be killed for one to be taken alive during capture by the slave-dealers.

The myth suited everybody: to speak of the 'greatest genocide in history' was for the Western colonialists to have their own crimes forgotten (the decimation of the American Indians and the African slave-trade), as it was a way for Stalin to mask his own ferocious repressions."

The Mail, *Maclean's*, October 26, 1998
"The real reasons why, after 1492, Western Europe began a trajectory, dramatically outpacing China and the world of Islam in wealth creation and in political liberty: superior weapons, disease, slavery, and two new, recently depopulated continents to plunder."

U.S. Sponsored Assassinations

William Blum, *Killing Hope*

Following is a list of prominent foreign individuals whose assassination (or planning for the same) the United States has been involved in since the end of the Second World War (several assassinations in various parts of the world carried out by anti-Castro Cubans employed by the CIA and headquartered in the United States are not included):

1949—Kim Koo, Korean opposition leader; 1950s—Numerous political figures in West Germany; 1950s—Chou En-lai, Prime minister of China; 1950s—Sukarno, President of Indonesia; 1951—Kim Il Sung, Premier of North Korea; 1950s—Claro M. Recto, Philippines opposition leader; 1955—Jawaharlal Nehru, Prime Minister of India; 1957—Gamal Abdul Nasser, President of Egypt; 1959—Norodom Sihanouk, leader of Cambodia; 1960—Brig. Gen. Abdul Karim Kassem, leader of Iraq; 1950s to 1970s José Figueres, President of Costa Rica; 1961—Francois "Papa Doc" Duvalier, leader of Haiti; 1961—Patrice Lumumba, Prime Minister of the Congo; 1961—Gen. Rafael Trujillo, leader of Dominican Republic; 1963—Ngo Dinh Diem, President of South Vietnam ; 1960s—Fidel Castro, President of Cuba, many attempts on his life; 1960s—Raúl Castro, high official in government of Cuba; 1965—Francisco Caamaño, Dominican Republic opposition leader; 1965 to 1966—Charles de Gaulle, President of France; 1967—Che Guevara, Cuban leader; 1970—Salvador Allende, President of Chile; 1970—Gen. Rene Schneider, Commander-in-Chief of Army, Chile; 1970s to 1981—General Omar Torrijos, leader of Panama; 1972—General Manuel Noriega, Chief of Panama Intelligence; 1975—Mobutu Sese Seko, President of Zaire; 1976—Michael Manley, Prime Minister of Jamaica; 1980 to 1986—Muammar Qaddafi, leader of Libya; 1982—Ayatollah Khomeini, leader of Iran; 1983—Gen. Ahmed Dlimi, Moroccan Army commander; 1983—Miguel d'Escoto, Foreign Minister of Nicaragua; 1984—Nine comandantes of the Sandinista National Directorate; 1985—Sheikh Mohammed Hussein Fadlallah, Lebanese Shiite leader (80 people killed in the attempt); 1991—Saddam Hussein, leader of Iraq.

[Assassinations list reprinted with permission of William Blum.]

The Crusades and Jihad

Huston Smith, *The Illustrated World's Religions,* p.168
"Muhammad adhered meticulously to the charter he forged for Medina, which—grounded as it was in the Koranic injunction, 'Let there be no compulsion in religion'—is arguably the first mandate for religious tolerance in human history."

Karen Armstrong, *Muhammad: A Biography of the Prophet,* p.165
"There are also Christians there who feel it their duty to live alongside the oppressed and the destitute and engage in a dedicated struggle for a just and decent society. It is in this light that we should consider the Islamic jihad, which Westerners usually translate as 'holy war.'"

Akbar S. Ahmed, *Living Islam,* p.64
"An eyewitness of the fourth Crusade was horrified: 'I Geoffrey de Ville Hardouin, Martial of the court of Champagne, am sure that since the creation of the universe, a plundering worse than this has not been witnessed.' Compare this to Mehmet the conqueror's entry when, with humility and awe, he fell to his knees, taking the dust from the floor and wiping it on his turban as an act of devotion. Christians here have a saying: 'Better the turban of a Turk than the tiara of the Pope.'"

"As for the unfortunate Jews, they would be massacred by the Christians on their way to the Crusades and massacred by them on their way back from the Crusades. Not surprisingly Muslims thought that here was a civilization doomed to barbarism and backwardness for ever."

John Haywood, *Atlas of World History,* p.48
"As an inducement the papacy offered Crusaders spiritual and legal privileges. most important of which was remission of penances due for sin. This was popularly interpreted as a guarantee of immediate entry into heaven if the Crusader were to die on the expedition."

Former U.S. president George Bush
"I'm delighted that I've been invited out here today to salute you, who, in my view, are doing the Lord's work."—"Bush Salutes U.S. Air Strikes on Iraq as 'Lord's work'," *AFP,* January 19, 2000

Sharia or Islamic Law

Feisal Abdul Rauf, Imam of Al-Fatah Mosque in New York City, writes in *Islam, a Sacred Law*:

"Centuries before the European notion of separation of Church and State...[Islamic jurists] recognized such a conceptual separation and divided the body of Shariah rules into two categories: **religious observances** and **worldly matters**. The first,... they observed to be beyond the scope of modification. The second [subject to interpretation] covers the following:

1. Criminal Law: This includes crimes such as murder, larceny, fornication, drinking alcohol, libel.

2. Family Law: This...covers marriage, divorce, alimony, child custody, inheritance.

3. Transactions: This covers property rights, contracts, rules of sale, hire, gift, loans and debts, deposits, partnerships, and damages."

"One of the most sensible definitions of the purposes of the Shariah," writes Imam Feisal, was given by Ibn al-Qayyim al-Jawziyyah who said:

"The foundation of the Shariah is wisdom and the safeguarding of people's interests in this world and the next. In its entirety it is justice, mercy and wisdom. Every rule which transcends justice to tyranny, mercy to its opposite, the good to the evil, and wisdom to triviality does not belong to the Shariah..."

According to Imam Feisal the sources of Shariah are, in order:

1. The Quran—God's Word revealed to Prophet Muhammad.

2. The Sunnah—practice and teachings of the Prophet.

3. Ijma—consensus of those in authority.

4. Qiyas—reason, logic, and opinion based upon analogy.

Imam Feisal describes seven other methods for deriving Islamic laws. These seven, plus ijma and qiyas, are collectively know as ijtihad or interpretation, and/or opinion based upon reason and logic.

Several schools of Shariah have evolved: Shafii, Hanbali, Hanafi, Maliki—the orthodox schools, and Jafari—the Shiite school. The Zaydis and Ibadis also have their own schools.

Shariah has much greater flexibility than is portrayed in the West, and may better protect society than does Western law.

The Truth About Islam

Islam means "submission to the Will of God." In its ethical sense Islam signifies "striving after the ideal." A Muslim is one who submits to the Will of God. "Islam" and "Muslim" derive from the same word as the Arabic for "peace." The traditional Muslim greeting is "Peace be unto you."

Islam offers hope for salvation to the righteous and God-fearing of all religions. Muslims believe in the Divine Revelations of many prophets including Abraham, Moses, Jesus, Muhammad, but do not believe that God assumed human form. The Quran, Muslims believe, is God's Word and Final Revelation to The Prophet Muhammad. Revealed over a period of twenty-three years, The Quran was compiled and distributed to distant lands within twenty-five years of The Prophet's death in 632 A.D. This is the only Quran recognized by Muslims.

Comprising laws, moral precepts, and narratives, The Quran's timeless text remains an inspiration and guide for more than one fifth of humanity. Together with The Quran, the epitome of Classical Arabic, Muslims lives are guided by the examples and sayings of The Prophet. Thousands of sayings have been attributed to The Prophet. Some are accepted as authentic; some traced to The Prophet's companions; some are the subject of debate. Some examples:

"The first thing created by God was the Intellect."
"The most excellent Jihad is that for the conquest of self."
"The ink of the scholar is more holy than the blood of the martyr."
"One learned man is harder on the devil than a thousand ignorant worshippers."
"Riches are not from an abundance of worldly goods, but from a contented mind."
"Reflect upon God's creation but not upon His nature or else you will perish."
"He who wishes to enter Paradise at the best door must please his mother and father."
"No man is a true believer unless he desires for his brother that which he desires for himself."
"When the bier of anyone passes by you, whether Jew, Christian, or Muslim, rise to your feet."
"The thing which is lawful, but disliked by God, is divorce."
"Heaven lies at the feet of mothers."
"Women are the twin-halves of men."
"Actions will be judged according to intentions."
"That which is lawful is clear, and that which is unlawful likewise,
but there are certain doubtful things between the two from which it is well to abstain."
"The proof of a Muslim's sincerity is that he pays no attention to that which is not his business."
"That person is nearest to God, who pardons...him who would have injured him."
"Yield obedience to my successor, although he may be an Abyssinian slave."
"Assist any person oppressed, whether Muslim or non-Muslim."
"The creation is like God's family...the most beloved unto God
is the person who does good to God's family."
"Modesty and chastity are parts of the Faith."

Islamic Law is based upon The Quran, examples and sayings of The Prophet, consensus among the learned, analogical deduction, and individual reasoning. Islamic society comes closer than any other society to the ideal democracy. All persons are equal before God; goodness is the only criterion of worth. There is no priesthood in Islam; even a child, with greater knowledge of The Quran than his elders, may lead them in prayer. To become a Muslim one need only profess, "There is no god but God; Muhammad is the Messenger of God."

Ordering Information

Ask for *The War on Islam* (ISBN: 0–9700011–0–X) at your favorite book store. You may also use the coupon below to place your order:

Please send me _____ copies of *The War on Islam*. I enclose check drawn on a U.S. bank for $_____ computed as follows: $12.50 per copy, plus mailing and handling charge of $4.00 for the first copy, and $1.00 for each additional copy.

Name _____

Address _____

City _____ State _____ Zip_____

Mail completed coupon, and check made out to The Wisdom Fund, to:

The Wisdom Fund
Madrasah BooksDivision
P. O. Box 2723
Arlington, VA 22202
USA

Please allow 2 to 4 weeks for delivery. All sales are final.

For questions about your order or reseller discounts, please contact Madrasah Books—wisdom@twf.org.